GREAT WAR

D0530238

NORFOLK

Remembering 1914-18

NORFOLK
Remembering 1914–18

STEVE SMITH

The History Press

This book is dedicated to the men and women
of Norfolk who lived and served their county
in the Great War.

First published 2014

The History Press
The Mill, Brimscombe Port
Stroud, Gloucestershire, GL5 2QG
www.thehistorypress.co.uk

British Library Cataloguing in Publication Data.
A catalogue record for this book is available from the British Library.

ISBN 978 0 7509 5919 3

Typesetting and origination by The History Press
Printed in Great Britain

CONTENTS

TIMELINE

1914

4 August

Great Britain declares war on Germany

28 June

*Assassination of Archduke
Franz Ferdinand in Sarajevo*

23 August

Battle of Tannenberg commences

24 August

*The 1st Norfolks see action
at Mons, losing 250 men*

6 September

First Battle of the Marne

19 October

First Battle of Ypres

3 November

*The German Navy bombards
Great Yarmouth, causing slight damage*

1915

19 January

*The first Zeppelin raid targets
Great Yarmouth and King's Lynn*

February

*Norwich raises three Royal
Engineer Field Companies*

25 April

Allied landing at Gallipoli

7 May

Germans torpedo and sink the Lusitania

31 May

*First German Zeppelin
raid on London*

12 August

*The 5th Norfolks see action in
Gallipoli at Kuchuk Anafarta Ova*

25 September

*The 9th Norfolks
see action at Loos*

20 December

*Allies finish their evacuation of
and withdrawal from Gallipoli*

1916

24 January

The British Government introduces conscription

21 February

Battle of Verdun commences

29 April

Most of the 2nd Norfolks are captured after being besieged at Kut-al-Amara

31 May

Battle of Jutland

4 June

Brusilov Offensive commences

1 July

First Day of the Battle of the Somme: 57,000 British casualties

27 August

Italy declares war on Germany

The 8th Norfolks see action on the Somme at Montauban

18 December

Battle of Verdun ends

1917

6 April

The United States declares war on Germany

9 April

Battle of Arras

19 April

The 4th and 5th Norfolks see action at the Second Battle of Gaza

31 July

Third Battle of Ypres (Passchendaele)

20 August

Third Battle of Verdun

26 October

Second Battle of Passchendaele

20 November

Battle of Cambrai

The 7th Norfolks storm the Hindenburg Line at Cambrai

7 December

The United States declares war on Austria-Hungary

1918

3 March

Russia and the Central Powers sign the Treaty of Brest-Litovsk

21 March

Second Battle of the Somme

15 July

Second Battle of the Marne

5 August

The last Zeppelin raid is shot down off Wells

8 August

Battle of Amiens, first stage of the Hundred Days Offensive

22 September

The Great Allied Balkan victory

27 September

Storming of the Hindenburg Line

8 November

Armistice negotiations commence

9 November

Kaiser Wilhelm II abdicates, Germany is declared a Republic

11 November

Armistice Day, cessation of hostilities on the Western Front

14 November

The 9th Norfolks begin to march into Germany with the 6th Division

ACKNOWLEDGEMENTS

This book could not have been written without the help and support of my wife Claire and my daughters Lauren, Lily and Eden; all of them know that remembering the Great War is a passion for me. Secondly, to the three people I work closely with – Rosie, Simon and Clare – thank you for your patience and understanding when I have taken time off my day job to research and write this book!

A number of museums have helped with sources for this project, so thank you to Peter Billingham, John Smith, Tom Watson, Cedric Smith and Peter Pilgrim of Norfolk Constabulary Historical Collection; Nicola Hems, the curator of the Museum of the Broads; Megan Dennis of Gressinghall Farm and Workhouse; Alistair Murphy of Cromer Museum; Dave King of the William Marriott Museum and especially Sue White of Bishop Bonner's Cottage Museum, who contributed so much to this book. Support has also come from Clare Everitt of Picture Norfolk and Rosemary Dixon of the *Eastern Daily Press* (*EDP*) Archive. Further support and some excellent articles in support of the book also came from Sam Russell, ably supported by Steve Downes of the *EDP*. I would also like to thank the staff at the Norfolk Records Office for their patience when I bombarded them with document requests and questions!

Runton Parish Council (RPC), the Neville-Rolfe family and Alan Forsdick are also deserving of thanks, along with all the private contributors who allowed me to tell the story of their relatives or provided pictures for the book. They are: Mike and Muriel Fuller, Gerald Statham, Les Fisher, Nick Cobb, Steve Crisp, Gus Ives, Jim Marriage and Nathan Waring. I would also like to thank Maurice Morson for allowing me to quote from his book on Norwich City Police.

Finally, a big thank you goes to my friend Nick Stone who introduced me to my commissioning editor, Cate Ludlow, at The History Press; had it not been for that, then someone else may well have written this book!

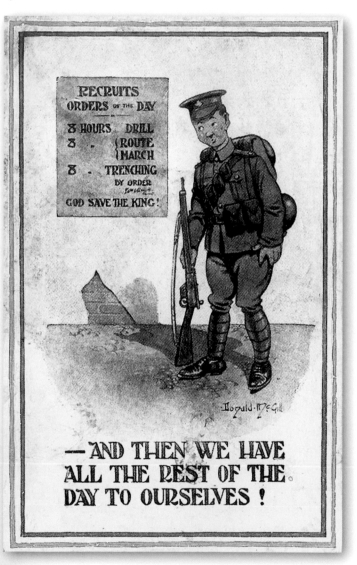

The lighter side of army life as seen in 1918. (Courtesy of Mike and Muriel Fuller)

INTRODUCTION

It gives me immense pleasure and pride to be allowed to write a book like this. It is hoped that the sacrifice made by the people of Norfolk is fully recognised within and it will be the experiences of Norfolk people in the Great War that bring this book to life.

At the time of the First World War, Norfolk – along with its capital, Norwich – was a county of market towns. Its local industries included quarrying, farming crops and livestock, and fishing, as well as producing exports of linens and clothing. In 1912, *Kelly's Directory of Norfolk* described it as a '… seacoast county, in the East of England, on the shores of the North Sea, close to the Great Wash; it took its name from the East English settlers, who called their people in these parts "North-Folk"…'. These 'North-Folk' were, and have always been, described as hardy and stout with a unique sense of humour and a simple way of life. But one of Norfolk's sons, Horatio Nelson, also captured their abiding sense of local pride when he said, 'I am a Norfolk man and Glory in being so.'

Norfolk's pre-war way of life would see great change as the events of 1914–18 began to unfold. On 28 June 1914, the assassination of Archduke Franz Ferdinand and his wife Sophie shocked the western world. This single act of terrorism in Sarajevo, meted out by a previously unremarkable individual – Gavrilo Princip – would lead to unthinkable consequences, plunging the world into its first global war with the various countries of Europe taking sides as they sought to settle old scores.

An initial belief that the war could be over by Christmas was soon revealed to be fantasy and the Great War would go on to reach a scale not seen in Europe since Napoleon was defeated at Waterloo in 1815.

Various talks were held in a bid to stop a new European war and Britain took an active role in trying to broker peace and avert the growing crisis. Despite all of this, Europe moved ever closer to war during the summer of 1914, with events escalating in a countdown to war that would take the lives of millions. On 4 August 1914, Britain could no longer avoid the conflict, declaring war on Germany following the invasion of neutral Belgium. The conflict would see Norfolk willingly send its sons and daughters to fight and serve in a war where many would not return and where countless thousands would see their lives changed forever.

1

OUTBREAK OF WAR

In the build-up to the outbreak of war, one celebrity family was on holiday in Norfolk. Clementine Churchill had been adamant that their children should have a holiday that summer and Winston Churchill, who was then First Lord of the Admiralty, would often come and spend his weekends at Pear Tree Cottage in Overstrand. Churchill used the telephone at the Sea Marge, the holiday home of

GREAT WAR BEGINS

GERMAN ARMIES IN FRANCE.

RUSSIAN ARMIES IN GERMANY.

GERMAN OCCUPATION OF LUXEMBURG

REPORTED GERMAN DEFEAT.

MR. ASQUITH WITH THE KING AT 2 A.M.

PREMIER'S STATEMENT TO-DAY.

CREDIT VOTE OF £50,000,000

The headline in the Eastern Daily Press *on 4 August 1914. (EDP)*

Edgar Speyer, to call the Admiralty to be kept abreast of the situation in Europe and the Balkans. However, as the crisis worsened, Churchill had to return to London, leaving his wife Clemmie at Overstrand to make the best of their remaining family holiday.

Sadly, the efforts made that summer to avert war were dashed when, on 2 August 1914, Germany launched the Schlieffen Plan in an attempt to defeat France quickly. Germany prepared for a rapid advance, declaring war against France at 6.45 p.m. on 3 August and invading neutral Luxembourg and Belgium on 4 August. To their surprise, however, the Belgian Army – who only had six infantry divisions, totalling 43,000 men – were able to hold up their advance. Further setbacks arose when Russia pre-empted a strike on her borders and began to move into East Prussia. Despite these obstacles, the German Army quickly overwhelmed Belgium's defence system and continued to move onwards.

Great Britain, following an ultimatum calling for Germany to withdraw her forces from neutral Belgium, also declared war on 4 August and fully mobilised her forces against Germany. The *Eastern Daily Press* (*EDP*) carried the headline 'GREAT WAR BEGINS' in bold capitals and the report beneath noted that, 'The great European war has commenced, Germany has invaded France. Russia has invaded Germany at several points. The date is a fateful one, as it was on August 2nd, 1870, that the first shots in the Franco-German War were fired.'

Captain Arthur Neville Rolfe, who would soon end up on the Western Front, was a Heacham man and serving with the 5th Gurkha Rifles when war commenced. He recorded his reaction to the news:

It must have been on 5 August 1914 that I was just going to drive off the 9th tee at Gulmarg, when a friend shouted out to me 'War's declared'. I can't remember whether I celebrated the event by driving into a bunker, but I do know that with the characteristic British phlegm, I finished the game, just as Drake had done several years before me.

Another man, known only as S.H.A., wrote of his experiences of this time whilst later recovering from wounds in Norfolk. At the outbreak of war he had found himself in Germany, where he was staying in Varel near Oldenberg. He was given twenty-four hours to leave and, as he made his way back, he was detained near Bremen:

> Soldiers met the train, and I was taken to a shed outside the station. I had left my heavy luggage, bringing only hand luggage with me. This they searched minutely, read all my letters etc. After some hours I was allowed to travel with a military pass; a German lady whom I knew travelled with me.

Luckily, S.H.A. was able to cross the border into Holland and returned to Britain via Rotterdam.

Norfolk on the eve of the Great War was a county that had become quite prosperous. In addition to agriculture and cloth, it was famed for exporting herring, and fishing was a big source of income for the coastal villages from Great Yarmouth to King's Lynn. It was also served by the Great Eastern and the Midland & Great Northern railways, since Norfolk was now a place to come to bathe and many people holidayed by the sea and on the Norfolk Broads.

Holidaying in Norfolk could, however, come with its risks in wartime Britain. The fear that spies were lurking around every corner was very tangible that summer and, on 13 August 1914, Clemmie Churchill was told that a cottager's wife had seen two men walking on a cliff path near Cromer who were acting suspiciously and speaking in a foreign language. The woman noted as they passed her that they had four carrier pigeons hidden in their coats. Keeping her distance, she followed them but they disappeared down a lane. The woman was able to alert two officers, who caught up with the men. Clemmie's daughter Mary later recounted the incident:

> Mother is much alarmed at the 'carrier pigeon story' and insists that the message carried by the pigeons was that 'the wife of the First Sea Lord is at Overstrand and that the Germans are to send an aeroplane to kidnap me and then I am to be ransomed by the handing over of several of our handsomest ships'.

Clemmie Churchill was not the only person to have concerns over suspicious activity at the outbreak of war. Henry Upcher of Sheringham Hall wrote to MP Oliver Locker-Lampson on 13 September 1914 about his reservations regarding a hotel manager:

> The Cromer lighthouse is not allowed to light up so the manager of the Links Hotel, a German, took upon himself to light up his hotel, especially the top of it, in the most brilliant way he possibly could. His home was surrounded by Territorials and searched from top to bottom and the lights extinguished.

A series of letters followed, whereby Henry Upcher explained the circumstances of the alleged spies in Cromer; these were passed on to the Admiralty after Locker-Lampson replied, stating, 'I hear the Hotel Manager in question is very much suspected already'. A further letter stated that, '… the matter will be satisfactorily dealt with'. Henry Upcher also provides an insight into the feelings shared by many of the residents of Norfolk at the outbreak of war when he noted in the same letter to Locker-Lampson:

> Now will you or some of the big guns in Parliament make it absolutely clear to the Government that our residents in Norfolk, though willing and ready to do something for our King and Country, have no intention of sitting down and allowing the lives of men, wives and children to be endangered …

Spies or no spies, the war preparations carried on regardless and, as a precaution against any German landing, the 11th Brigade from the 4th Division was sent to Cromer to defend the Norfolk coastline. Five cyclist battalions and the 2nd Mounted Division, a Yeomanry unit, were also sent to put mounted brigades at King's Lynn (1st South Midland), Fakenham (2nd South Midland) and Holt (Notts & Derby). Reservists were also quickly called up and the King's Proclamation – summoning men to defend

BY THE KING.
A PROCLAMATION
For Calling out Men of the Royal Naval Reserve and Royal Fleet Reserve, and Officers and Men of the Royal Naval Volunteer Reserve.

GEORGE R.I.

WHEREAS by the fourth section of the Royal Naval Reserve (Volunteer) Act, 1859, it is enacted that it shall be lawful for Us on such occasions as We shall deem fit (the occasion being first communicated to Parliament if Parliament be sitting or declared in Council and notified by Proclamation if Parliament be not sitting or in being) to order and direct that the Volunteers under that Act, or so many or such part of them as We may deem necessary, shall be called into actual service:

And whereas by the Royal Naval Reserve Volunteer Act, 1896, as amended by the Royal Naval Reserve Act, 1902, it is enacted that the power under the said Act of 1859 to raise and pay Volunteers may be exercised outside the British Islands in respect of British subjects:

And whereas by the Naval Reserve Act, 1900, the Admiralty are authorized to raise and keep up a new division, commonly known as the Royal Fleet Reserve, of the force raised under the said first recited Act in addition to the men raised under that Act, and such new division is liable to be called out as part of the Royal Naval Reserve under the said fourth section of the said Act of 1859:

And whereas by the Naval Forces Act, 1903, it is provided that the Admiralty may raise and maintain a force to be called the Royal Naval Volunteer Reserve, and that certain provisions of the said Act of 1859 (including the fourth section of that Act) as amended by any subsequent enactment shall apply to the force so raised:

And whereas by the first section of the Naval Reserve (Mobilisation) Act, 1900, amending the said Act of 1859, it is enacted that it shall be lawful for Us where We order and direct that Volunteers under that Act shall be called into actual service to authorize the Admiralty to give and, when given, to revoke or vary such directions as may seem necessary or proper for calling out all or any of the said Volunteers as the occasion may require:

And whereas Parliament is not sitting:

And whereas We have declared in Council and hereby notify that owing to the state of Public Affairs and the demands upon Our Naval Forces for the protection of the Empire an occasion has arisen for ordering and directing as in the said Act provided:

WE DO by this Our Proclamation order and direct that Volunteers under the said Acts shall be called into actual service:

AND WE do hereby authorize the said Lords Commissioners of the Admiralty to give and, when given, to revoke or vary such directions as may seem necessary or proper for calling out all or any of the said Volunteers as the occasion may require.

Given at Our Court at Buckingham Palace, this Third day of August, in the year of our Lord one thousand nine hundred and fourteen, and in the Fifth year of Our Reign.

GOD SAVE THE KING.

their country – was displayed throughout the locality. From 5 August 1914, before war was even officially declared, men in the Royal Navy had their service period extended, members of the Royal Naval Reserve were called up and the Admiralty was given the power to requisition ships.

Norfolk's Battalions

The two regular battalions of the Norfolk Regiment went to war very early on. The first of these, serving under the command of Lieutenant Colonel Colin Robert Ballard, was the 1st Battalion who were stationed at Holywood in Belfast, serving with the

The 1/6th Battalion Norfolk Regiment at Westwick Camp in 1914 – including Augustus Ives, who appears second left. (Courtesy of Gus Ives)

15th Brigade in the 5th Division. The other was the 2nd Battalion, under the command of Lieutenant Colonel E.C. Peebles, who were serving at Belgaum in India and were part of the 18th (Belgaum) Brigade in the 6th (Poona) Division of the Indian Army.

The first man to die serving with the Norfolks was a soldier from the 2nd Battalion; this was Private 8117 William Richard Westbrook, who died of tuberculosis on 17 August 1914. Both battalions were mobilised quite quickly and it was the 1st Battalion who would be involved in the first major battles of the war. They landed in France on 16 August 1914 as part of the British Expeditionary Force (BEF) of six infantry and one cavalry division, under the command of Field Marshal Sir John French. The departure of the 15th Brigade was recorded by their historian as a, 'great waving of handkerchiefs and cheering as we warped slowly out of Belfast docks at 3 P.M. and moved slowly down the channel.'

The BEF moved rapidly towards the Germans and this swift advance was one of the things that ultimately thwarted the Schlieffen Plan. The BEF was not a large body of men – only totalling 80,000 men – and, as a result, the French commander-in-chief, Joseph Joffre, had placed this small but highly trained army on his left flank, where he believed there would not be much fighting. The plan called for the French to take the brunt of the German Army, but in the event they were bloodily repulsed. The advance of the BEF, meanwhile, was stopped on 23 August at the Mons-Conde Canal and this is where their first major battle took place. This was the Battle of Mons and it was here that the British 1st and 2nd Corps met the German 1st Army commanded by General Von Kluck.

On 18 August, the 15th Brigade had arrived at Le Cateau and by 22 August they were at the Bois de Bossu, where they went into the reserve with the 13th and 14th Brigades positioned along the canal. It was on this day, the 22nd, that the 1st Battalion Norfolk Regiment lost their first man. Private 6271 William Porter was born in Shouldham and first enlisted on 9 September 1902 at the age of 19 years and 11 months. He left the regular army in 1905 but in 1914 he was asked to extend his time in the army reserve and was called to action as a member of the 1st Battalion. Following the Battle of Mons he was listed as missing and later an official statement was issued confirming that William Porter had '… died on or since 22-8-14'. He was married to Florence Porter and had two children: Leslie and William. He has no known grave and is commemorated on the La Ferte-sous-Jouarre Memorial.

The Battle of Mons, on 23 August 1914, saw the British fielding around 70,000 men and 300 artillery pieces, fighting against 160,000 men and 600 artillery pieces on the German side. The Germans vied to cross the canal in order to capture the main bridges there. Although the BEF was a professional body of men who were well trained, they had no hope of holding Mons and by 1 p.m. they were retreating before the Germans, who had managed to cross the canal and gain footholds. The French Army was also capitulating in other sectors and the BEF ran the risk of being outflanked on both sides as the Germans gained ground. Retreat was the only option and the order to do so was given by Field Marshal French in the early evening. At this point the 1/Norfolks had not seen any offensive action and would not do so until 24 August, when they were ordered to Dour with the 1/Cheshires and the 119th Battery Royal Field Artillery to act as the reserve. The 13th and 14th Brigades were now withdrawing and, through an error made by other units, it was found that the left flank of the 5th Division was threatened. As a result, the 1/Norfolks and the 1/Cheshires – under the command of Lieutenant Colonel Ballard – were ordered to advance north in a counter-attack, and they ended up along the Elouge-Audregnies-Angre road supported by the 2nd and 3rd Cavalry Brigades, who were in the vicinity of Audregnies.

At 12.30 p.m., with Ballard's force securing touch with the cavalry, the Germans struck from the direction of Quievrain, the Bois de Deduit and Baisieux. The 2nd Cavalry Brigade were ordered to attack and did so; they sustained heavy casualties but this gave Ballard's force time to position itself as flank guard. The Germans, advancing from the direction of Quievrain, were met with fire from L Battery while 119 Battery fired upon the German artillery. Meanwhile, the Norfolks fired upon German infantry who were streaming out of Quievrain and the Cheshires turned their attention to enemy forces coming from the direction of Bois de Deduit. Sadly, this was not enough; Ballard was given reports that an entire German army corps was moving to the south and he ordered a retreat at 2.30 p.m. The Norfolks fell back in two parties and had to leave 100 of their wounded at Elouges.

Ballard's troops managed to withdraw towards Audregnies, where they dislodged the Germans from their vantage point before being surrounded and overwhelmed around Athis. It was the gunners of the 5th Division who succeeded in stopping the German advance, allowing the survivors of Ballard's force to reach their muster point at St Waast. The history of the 15th Brigade recorded:

Just beyond Athis we found the Norfolks, who had been fighting at Élouges all the morning, and then we came across the sad little remainder of the Cheshires – only about 200 left out of 891 who had gone into action that morning near Élouges …

In this action the Norfolks had lost over 250 men, of which fifty-four officers and men were killed in action. Many Norfolk men died in other regiments during this stage of the war – one example being Frederick Leach who was killed in action serving with the 16/Lancers on 12 September 1914. He had been shot in the stomach whilst looking for the enemy in Venizel and a letter to his father stated, 'We got into the village later that day but found Pte Leach had only lived ½ hour after being picked up and he was lying in one of the French houses.'

It was not long before the 2/Norfolks were in action as well. This force left Belgaum on 6 November on board *Elephanta* before heading for the Persian Gulf and Mesopotamia. Great Britain initially sent a force to protect the oil refineries at Abadan and to seize control of Mesopotamia, which would allow wider access into the Middle East. This would pitch them against the Ottoman Empire, who were allied with Germany.

Just prior to sailing, Private 8293 Frank Wheeler wrote to his mother and said, '… don't worry if I am unable to come back and if not you will know I have done my duty as far as I am able for King and Country so tell them all to keep a light heart.' Frank landed with the rest of the battalion at Saniyah on 15 November 1914. They went into action two days later when the advance came up against opposition at an old fort and the village of Sahil. Here the Norfolks, the 2/Dorsets and the 7/Rajputs advanced on a Turkish trench, taking the left flank and coming under heavy rifle and shrapnel fire. This caused substantial numbers of casualties but eventually the Turkish defenders were driven from the trench and most of those that fled were killed by artillery.

Although the advance was hampered by a Turkish gun, support was provided by the Royal Navy and part of the front was shaded by palms. Following this, the 2/Norfolks went into a camp 1 mile south of the fort and spent a very uncomfortable night in the cold being sniped at. The next day the troops set about discovering these snipers and B Company found a deserted enemy camp. They assisted in clearing up the area on 19 and 21 November and found fifteen

The 1911 Census for Norwich, Great Yarmouth, King's Lynn and Thetford boroughs produced a total of 601,339 inhabitants with 700 civil parishes. The population for the main market towns were: Aylsham 2,627, Cromer 4,073, East Dereham 5,729, Diss 3,769, Downham Market 2,497, Fakenham 3,181, Swaffham 3,234, North Walsham 4,254, Wells-next-Sea 2,565, Wymondham 4,794.

Private 8293 Frank Wheeler 2/Norfolks. (Author's collection)

of the 2/Dorsets dead before embarking on the SS *Medjidieh*, which was going to Basra.

Sadly, Frank Wheeler had been seriously wounded in the arms and was evacuated to a field hospital, where he died of his wounds on 18 November. His company commander, Captain Robert Marshall, wrote to Wheeler's mother on 29 November and said, 'I am exceedingly sorry to lose such a good lad and popular with his comrades. He was buried on the 18th Nov and

Gen Sir Arthur Barrett, Gens Fry and Robinson, the Colonel and officers of the battalion being present.'

The War Strikes Home

These actions, taking place on the front lines of the war, would have seemed quite distant to the inhabitants of Norfolk. However, the war would land on Norfolk's doorstep twice very early on in the conflict. The first incident occurred at 7.00 a.m. on 3 November 1914, when two raiding groups from the German Navy appeared off the coast of Great Yarmouth.

Known as the 1st and 2nd Scouting Group and led by Admiral Franz von Hipper, the battle cruisers SMS *Seydlitz*, *Von der Tann* and *Moltke*, the cruiser SMS *Blücher* and the light cruisers SMS *Strassburg*, *Graudenz*, *Kolberg* and *Stralsund* steadily approached the British coast. The raid had a number of objectives: to lay mines off the coast of Great Yarmouth and Lowestoft, to sink any ships found and to entice a larger enemy force of ships to chase them into a trap, where the German High Seas Fleet was waiting for them. The raiders were also tasked with firing on Great Yarmouth.

SMS Seydlitz *raided Great Yarmouth on 3 November 1914. (Author's collection)*

The enemy vessels were spotted by minesweeper HMS *Halcyon* – a Dryad-class torpedo gunboat patrolling off Great Yarmouth – who challenged the ships and was fired upon, causing slight damage and wounding three of her crew. Two destroyers, HMS *Lively* and *Leopard*, laid a smoke screen and joined the action. The heavy fire directed at the Royal Navy ships was inaccurate due to the smoke screen and, in the excitement, the Germans failed to correct their aim. At 7.40 a.m., once SMS *Stralsund* had managed to lay 100 mines off Smith's Knoll, Admiral Hipper turned his attention to Great Yarmouth. The ships directed their shells at the town but most of these landed on Gorleston Beach, completely short of their intended target. A number of fishermen witnessed this action and, in an account from the time, stated, '… some hundred and twenty shots were fired. The fishermen in the first instance mistook them for British ships and one man, as they passed close by, waved a friendly teapot at them; to which the German sailors replied by shaking their fists.'

HMS *Halcyon* was able to alert the mainland and HMS *Success* joined the battle with three other destroyers and three submarines – *D3*, *D5* and *D10* – moving out to meet the enemy. Sadly, *D5* struck a mine with the loss of twenty-four crew and only five survivors. By the time any reactive force could be coordinated, the German raiders were 50 miles away and on their way home. The raid on Great Yarmouth prompted the War Office to bolster Norfolk's sea defences between Salthouse and Briston, including the digging of trenches, and elements of the Royal Field Artillery were put into positions between Weybourne and Gorleston.

The second incident came as a result of the Kaiser's sanction – at the beginning of 1915 – of the bombing of military and industrial targets along the British coast and in the area around the Thames Estuary (though not London itself). Therefore, on 19 January 1915, Zeppelins L3, L4 and L6 of the Imperial German Navy, under the overall command of Zeppelin commander Korvettenkapitän Peter Strasser, took off from their base at Fuhlsbüttel in Germany and were to attack military and industrial buildings on Humberside. L6,

Zeppelin L3 attacked Great Yarmouth on 19 January 1915. (Author's collection)

which carried Strasser, encountered mechanical problems and bad weather caused it to turn back. Weather also had a bearing on the two remaining airships, which had to change their plans and eventually made landfall in Norfolk, where L3 turned south-east towards Great Yarmouth and Zeppelin L4 flew north-west towards Kings Lynn.

Zeppelin L3, under the command of Kapitänleutnant Hans Fritz, crossed the Norfolk coast between Happisburgh and Winterton, officially being first spotted near Ingham, and navigated its way towards Great Yarmouth. A total of ten incendiary and high-explosive bombs would fall there in the space of ten minutes. This included one that fell on St Peter's Plain where spinster Martha Taylor and shoemaker Samuel Smith became the first civilians to be killed in an air raid. Damage would be caused to houses, the South Dock, the Fish Wharf and a steam drifter. Zeppelin L4,

Prior to the First World War, there were more male than female births. Between 1891 and 1901, the birth rate in Norwich increased by 10.7 per cent. By 1908, infant mortality in the first year of life had dropped to 125 per 1,000 births through the implementation of a number of health and social care policies.

under the command of Kapitänleutnant Count Magnus von Platen-Hallermund, navigated the Norfolk coast.

One witness to this attack was Captain Neville-Rolfe, who had been wounded in December 1914 and was recovering at home in Heacham. He remembered that:

This house in St Peter's Plain was destroyed in the first raid. The man inside was unhurt but 72-year-old Martha Taylor was killed as she walked to fetch her dinner. Samuel Smith was killed by a second bomb that landed nearby. They were the first British victims of an air raid on the home front. (The Illustrated War News)

Towards the end of January I was woken one night by what sounded like twenty motor cycles charging down a neighbouring hill, but proved to be the first Zeppelin raid on England. The airship, flying very low, crossed coast at our village, giving Heacham the distinction of receiving the first bomb ever dropped on English soil. It was an incendiary and appropriately dropped into a washerwoman's soft water butt. What she said about 'them there Jarmans' might have stopped the war had the Kaiser heard it. The second bomb was a 50 kilo H.E. which did not explode.

Sadly, Heacham cannot lay claim to this fact because by then L4 had dropped bombs on Sheringham, Brancaster-Staithe and Brancaster prior to attacking Heacham and Snettisham. L4 eventually reached King's Lynn where more fatalities were caused at Bentinck Road, with a bomb killing Percy Goate, aged 14, and Alice Gazely, aged 26. Both are reported to have died from shock and, in total, the raid on King's Lynn injured thirteen others. After the raid, L4 headed east and actually flew past Norwich, which was luckily shrouded in fog and had its lights out, and then was seen to pass Acle before flying out to sea to the north of Great Yarmouth. Of all the accounts I have read of the raid, the most outspoken has to be the borough coroner, J. Tolver Waters, who – although declaring that the raid on Great Yarmouth was murder – knew this could not be the verdict given by the jury. In his closing summary he stated:

Two of the bombs that fell on 19 January. The first shows an unexploded bomb at Yarmouth, and the second shows another bomb – too heavy for a single man to lift – which fell into a stable and became lodged in the straw. The animal inside the stable was not harmed. (The Illustrated War News)

The unfortunate man and woman were victims of so-called warfare, but I do not call it so. It is the offspring of German culture. It is contrary to International Law to attack any unfortified place, such as Yarmouth is. But the Germans are past masters of regarding anything in the form of writing as a mere scrap of paper.

Zeppelin L4 also flew over Sandringham. Propaganda suggested that the Royal Family were the chief targets of this attack but, in actual fact, they were not in residence that night. In a letter to Lord Fisher, Queen Alexandra noted:

Another view of the houses in Bentinck Street in which Percy and Mrs Gazeley died. (The Illustrated War News)

This is too bad, those beasts actually went straight to Sandringham. I suppose in the hopes of exterminating us with their Zeppelin bombs, though thank God, they failed this time. But they killed and wounded as usual a poor lot of innocent women and children at King's Lynn, I am sorry to say.

The letter goes on to request that rockets with spikes or hooks are sent or invented '… to defend the Norfolk coast.'

The raid of January 1915 was discussed at a national level and the press went out of their way to vilify the Zeppelin crews as 'Baby Killers' with *The War Illustrated* reporting on 30 January 1915 that: 'The amount of damage done was small – no more than has happened often in a gas explosion – the loss of life slight; but loathsome blood-mad fiends who could do this foul work and rejoice stirred every Briton's heart to sterner resolve …' The article continued, 'Germany is gloating over the proof that their Zeppelins can cross the North Sea and kill English children of four years old and English women of seventy.' In reality, no children aged 4 died in the raids on King's Lynn and Yarmouth and it just shows how certain truths can be twisted to suit a specific aim.

The result of the German raid on Norfolk. Top left shows the crater left at the royal station by a bomb, while bottom left shows another crater near the church at Snettisham, the explosion of which blew out many of the church's windows. The image on the right shows the ruins of the houses in which Percy Goate and Mrs Gazeley were killed. (The Illustrated War News)

The chief constable of King's Lynn examining an unexploded bomb that fell through a house. (The Illustrated War News, *Norfolk Constabulary Historical Collection*)

Zeppelin Bomb dropped on Heacham.

Mrs. Gazeley, killed by a Zeppelin bomb, and husband who died fighting at the front.

PC 78 Brookes standing with soldiers and onlookers guarding a bomb dropped by Zeppelin L4 on Heacham. (Norfolk Constabulary Historical Collection)

Alice Gazeley and her husband Percy. (The War Illustrated)

31

CHARLIE FREDERICK COBB

Charlie Frederick Cobb was born in Gaywood on 9 August 1898. He enlisted on 7 September 1914, joining the 2/5th Norfolk Regiment – a reserve Territorial Force (TF) battalion which was being formed at Dereham at that time. Charlie's service record shows that medically he was fit and was described as 5ft 5in tall with a 33½in chest. On his enlistment papers Charlie listed his age as 18, but in reality he had only just turned 16. By January 1915, Charlie was serving with D Company, No. 3 Section.

On 23 October 1915, whilst stationed at Bury St Edmunds, Charlie signed his Imperial and General Service Obligation which would render him liable to service overseas. On 3 December 1916, he was posted to France, landing at Boulogne, and he became a draft for the 9/Norfolks, where he served with No. 9 Platoon in C Company.

Charlie's mother wrote two letters to the War Office in December 1916 once she had heard this news and in the second letter she stated, 'I hope that you will do what you can to stop him from going to the trenches.'

By 21 January 1917 he was back in England, where he transferred to the 2nd Battalion King's Own Scottish Borderers and, by 16 October 1917, he had returned to France where, seven days later, he was awarded Field Punishment No. 1 for irregular conduct with regards to dividing the rations. He served in Italy but, by March 1918, his battalion was back in France where Charlie would have seen much of the terrible fighting that took place towards the end of the war, including the final advance in Picardy. Luckily, Charlie survived the war, including a bout of influenza, and was discharged from the army on 14 March 1919.

The 2/5th Norfolk Regiment marching through Peterborough with Charlie Cobb amongst them. (Courtesy of Nick Cobb)

2

PREPARATIONS AT HOME

At the start of hostilities, as we have already seen, the county had two regular battalions of the Norfolk Regiment serving in other parts of the world. But the Norfolk Regiment also had the 3rd (Reserve) Battalion, who were based at Britannia Barracks in Norwich, as well as the Territorial Force (TF) units, which were volunteer battalions. Part of this force was the East Anglian Division, the units of which were on their annual

Troops leaving Norwich Station (Gressingham Museum)

summer camp when war was declared, so emergency orders were sent to recall them. By 5 August 1914, they were fully mobilised for full-time war service and by 20 August the entire division was positioned around Chelmsford, Bury St Edmunds and Norwich.

The TF was designed to be a home force but could be used for overseas service should crisis erupt in the Empire. It officially came to be on 1 April 1908 and Norfolk raised three infantry battalions – the 1/4th, 1/5th and 1/6th (Cyclists), as well as one cavalry battalion (the King's Own Royal Regiment of Norfolk Yeomanry) and various units that would support the main battalions such as the reserve battalions, field ambulance, artillery and service corps.

Before long the Regular Army needed to be expanded and, as part of a national decision made by Field Marshal Earl Kitchener of Khartoum, a further three regular Norfolk battalions were raised. The 7th (Service) Battalion became part of the 35th Brigade in the 12th (Eastern) Division under the command of Lieutenant Colonel John W.V. Carroll. Next came the 8th (Service) Battalion, who joined the 53rd Brigade in the 18th (Eastern) Division initially under the command of Colonel Frederick C. Briggs, and finally the 9th (Service) Battalion, who joined the 71st Brigade in the 24th Division under the command of Lieutenant Colonel Ernest Stracey.

What is not as widely known is that three Royal Engineer Field Companies were also formed by the Lord Mayor of Norwich, Dr Gordon Munn, who raised these 'New Army' units in February 1915. These were the 207th, 208th and 209th Field Companies who would go on to serve with the ill-fated 34th Division. They were three 'pals' units and evidence shows, as in similar cases across the country, that men from similar areas or similar lines of work would often join up together and were initially encouraged to do so. A prime example would be five police officers from Norwich City Police who joined up together: William Thomas Green, Harry Hazel, William Jinks, Herbert James Whitchand and Henry Crisp, who all originally served in 208 Field Company Royal Engineers.

Officers of the 34th Division Field Companies in 1915. (Picture Norfolk)

Norwich City Police Officer William Thomas Green. (Picture Norfolk)

The Norfolk Constabulary records show that these five policemen all joined up on 7 June 1915 with army service numbers which fall between 85502 and 85592. Since these service numbers were sequential it is almost certain that these men joined together, with just ninety numbers between Green and Crisp joining up. Perhaps spurred on by the action of these men, three other police officers from Norwich also joined the 208th Field Company. On 8 June 1915, William Sawford Andrew enlisted and was given the service number 85549, while on 14 July 1915, Henry Crisp joined up as number 85595. Finally, Arthur Bell enlisted on 14 August 1915 and received service number 85666. Between 28 and 31 August 1915, the entire division moved to Salisbury Plain and camped around Sutton Veny near Warminster, where they carried out some final training and practised live firing. Albert Statham, who worked for the General Post Office (GPO) in Norwich, also enlisted with the Royal Engineers on 24 September 1915 and found himself in the 34th Division's Signals. The 34th Division embarked for France on 8 January 1916.

Along with 'pals' joining up to do their bit, it was often the case that several members of the same family would take part in the war effort. The Cobb family provide an example of this. The family came from Gaywood and Henry and Keren Cobb had six children, four of whom joined up. William, the eldest son, went to Australia and, by 1 October 1915, he was serving with the 23rd Company, Australian Army Service Corps. Harry, the second eldest son, initially served in one of the Norfolk TFs before joining the 2/6th Battalion Gloucestershire Regiment, while his sister Gladys joined the Queen Mary's Army Auxiliary Corp as an Ordinary Worker and was seconded to the Royal Engineers at Richborough. Finally the youngest brother, Charley, joined up underage – having just turned 16 – and initially served with the 2/5th Norfolk Regiment.

On 6 August 1914, by order of Field Marshal Earl Kitchener of Khartoum, Parliament sanctioned an increase of 500,000 men in the Regular Army, all recruited from volunteers. By 21 August 1914, Army Order 324 reported the formation of six new divisions in Kitchener's Army, known as K1.

Joining Up Together

One of the best examples of friends joining up together can be found in the case of six men who sang together in the Billingford Church Choir. Enlisting in Norwich on 11 November 1914, their army service numbers are only ten digits apart.

- Private 16361 Allen Race served with the 2/Norfolks, landing in Basrah on 7 February 1916. He survived the war and was discharged from the army on 10 November 1919.
- Private, later corporal, 16366 Herbert Race landed in France as a draft on 4 October 1915. He served with the 9/Norfolks and was killed in action on 1 April 1917 while the battalion was at St Elie near Loos. He was 23 years old, the son of George and Rosa Race of Billingford and the brother of Allan. He is now laid to rest in Philosophe British Cemetery.
- Private 16367 John Lewis Whiting, grandson of James and Mary Batley, was born in Stepney and served in the 2/Norfolks. He died in India on 9 May 1917 and is commemorated on the Kirkee 1914–18 memorial.
- Private 16368 Samuel Fisher initially served in the Norfolk Regiment before transferring to the Machine Gun Corps. He landed in France on 11 August 1915 as a draft and survived the war.
- Private 16370 Allan Fox was born in Billingford and landed in France as a draft on 12 August 1915 serving with the 9/Norfolks. Allan was killed in action on 21 March 1918 on the first day of the last German offensive of the First World War. The son of Jeremiah and Jessie Fox, he has no known grave and is commemorated on the Arras Memorial.
- Private 16371 Leonard Wilfred Bloomfield landed in Mesopotamia on 13 October 1915, serving with the 2/Norfolks, and also saw service in Egypt and France with the 6th Battalion Royal Dublin Fusiliers.

A traditional songbook. (Courtesy of Davide Restivo)

Joining Up

Men joined up either by enlisting or by receiving a commission. Enlistment often followed recruitment meetings, such as the one held at St Andrew's Hall, Norwich in August 1914. These kind of recruitment drives took place all over the county and soldiers' records show that they also enlisted in towns such as Great Yarmouth, Dereham and King's Lynn. In order to be accepted, men had to be physically fit and a stringent medical examination was held which could bar men who fell outside of the height requirements or had bad teeth. However, as the war progressed and casualties mounted, the medical requirements for recruits were often lowered.

Age was also a barrier and only men aged between 18 and 35 were accepted. This too changed as the war progressed, with the maximum age rising to 50 if the applicant had already served as an NCO. The fact that underage boys were joining the war effort was not widely known at the beginning of the war but there is evidence that this did happen.

Recruits marching down Unthank Road in Norwich in 1914. (Picture Norfolk)

John Norton, who joined the Norfolk Regiment underage, records how he managed to enlist with the help of a recruiting sergeant who was prepared to turn a blind eye: 'I was only sixteen, but I tried to join up too. The recruiting sergeant asked me my age and when I told him he said, "You better go out, come in again, and tell me different." I came back, told him I was nineteen and I was in.' Norton would go on to serve in the 8/Norfolks.

Those men who did not join up straight away often found themselves being forced to do so by other means, including public shaming. Clifford De Boltz was given a white feather in the street (the white feather became a symbol of cowardice given to those who seemed eligible to participate in the war effort but had yet to join up) and recalled, 'I felt quite embarrassed and threw the feather away in great disgust.' But it did the trick because he joined the 2/6th Norfolks, a cyclist battalion, and eventually went on to serve as an officer with the 1/Norfolks.

For those who were suitable to be commissioned, which at the start of the war often depended on your education or standing in life, the path to joining the army was quite different. At the start of the war, the position of officer was oversubscribed and a number of men were unable to register in this role as a result or else because they did not fit in with the regiment's requirements. Phillip Hewetson, the son of William Hewetson, rector of Hoveton, encountered this issue when he went to London to join the London Rifle Brigade.

When his request drew blank faces from the officer committee, Hewetson ascertained that no papers had been sent or that his papers had been lost. With no recommendation, which was often a requirement of a regiment, he was stuck: 'They showed us the list and said that was all the subalterns they would want, they were sorry as they supposed we wanted to keep together, still they were full so "Good morning" and we went!' Luckily, Hewetson found that an old friend, 'Comber', had heard of his

> The age of enlistment was initially set at between 18 and 30. It increased to 35 and was eventually raised to the age of 50 for those who had served previously. On 11 September 1914, Army Order 382 called for another 100,000 men to enlist. K2 and K3 of Kitchener's Army would soon be formed.

bad news and had recommended him to a general who knew of a colonel who was looking for subalterns to help to form a 'New Army' regiment. Eventually he obtained his commission in the Loyal North Lancashire Fusiliers.

There were many problems with this initial rush to join the colours and the influx of men meant that regiments were often unable to obtain the quantities of equipment and weapons necessary for the force to be sent overseas. Major H.P. Berney-Ficklin, who served with the 8/Norfolks, noted the preliminary issues faced as the battalion formed: 'The conditions in England at this time were practically indescribable. Men appeared in thousands … all in civilian clothes and had to be found accommodation, food, cooking utensils and boots; and had at the time to be taught the first principles in soldiering.'

A letter printed in the *EDP* on 3 September 1914 revealed another issue in the form of the distances that Norfolk men had to travel in order to enlist. As a result, Lord Kitchener appointed Lord Suffield of Hardbord House, Cromer; Colonel C.B. Custance, of Weston Hall, Norwich; and the Hon. William Cozens Hardy of Letheringsett Hall, Holt as special recruiting agents for the army, announcing that:

> Any village agent for recruiting who may have men who wish to enlist should communicate with the nearest recruiting officer or special recruiting agents at once, so that arrangements can be immediately made for examination and attestation of recruits as near their [home town] as possible.

By 4 September, around 250 recruits for the 8/Battalion had arrived at St Martin's Plain. Within eleven days this number had increased to 1,200 and by 20 September the battalion had a complement of 1,320 officers and men. The battalion was sent to Shorncliffe in Kent and initially men had to share cutlery and plates and were put in accommodation of sixteen men per tent. A number of men had to wear a blue uniform rather than khaki, some had no boots and a shortage of places for men to wash

YOUR KING AND
COUNTRY NEED YOU!

Sincerely Yours
William G. Collins.
26th November 1914

A cartoon depicting enlistment dated 26 November 1914. (Courtesy of Mike and Muriel Fuller)

meant that the entire battalion was regularly marched down to the sea. Rifles also remained in short supply, even when the battalion moved to Colchester, and it was not until June 1915 that the battalion could be considered fully operational.

Clifford De Boltz spent his first night as a recruit sleeping on a pub billiard table because the 2/6 Norfolks just could not cope with the number of men it had in its ranks. It had difficulties issuing uniforms and De Boltz noted, '… whether it fitted or not did not seem to matter to them but we all felt very uncomfortable. Boots, asked for size 5. CQMS "We haven't got any bloody boys' boots, take these size 7 and wear three pairs of socks and you will be alright."'

Priorities for the Norfolk TF men can be seen in a letter written by Harry Cobb in 1915 whilst still stationed in Norfolk:

Send handkerchiefs and towels when clean with socks. Don't send shirt. I have all I want bar the socks, handkerchiefs and towels, and also send my map of Norfolk if you can find it. It is not settled on whether we go to the coast on Friday or Saturday so don't send until you hear the address from me and send per return … Have been doing warfare field work and sham fighting this last three days.

The Billingford Church Choir boys, who all enlisted together. (Author's collection)

The men who joined up were very optimistic and often looked at enlistment as a way of getting away from their harsh lives and as a chance for adventure. One man who joined the

Members of Billingford Church Choir
1914
Top left - John Whiting, A. Race. H. Race
Bottom left - Sam Fisher, Leonard Bloomfield. Allan Fox

Westwick Camp.

THERE'S an isolated, desolated spot I'd like to mention,
  Where all you hear is "Stand at Ease," "Slope Arms,"
    "Quick March," "Attention,"
It's miles away from anywhere, by Gad, it is a rum'un,
A chap lived there for fifty years and never saw a woman.

There's only two lamps in the place, so tell it to your mother,
The postman carries one, and the policeman has the other,
And if you want a jolly night, and do not care a jot,
You take a ride upon the car, the car they haven't got.

There are lots of little huts, all dotted here and there,
For those who have to live inside, I've offered many a prayer,
Inside the huts, there's RATS as big as any Nanny Goat,
Last night a soldier saw One Fitting on his Overcoat.

For Breakfast every morning, just like Old Mother Hubbard,
You Double round the bloomin' Hut and jump up at the cupboard
Sometimes you get bacon, and sometimes "lively" cheese,
That forms Platoon upon your plate, Orders Arms and Stands
    at Ease.

It's dust up to the eyebrows, you get it in your ears,
But into it you've got to go without a sign of fear,
And when you've had a bath of dust, you just set to and groom,
And get cleaned up for next Parade, or else it's "Orderly Room."

Week in, week out, from morn till night, with full Pack and a rifle,
Like Jack and Jill, you climb the hills, of course that's just a trifle,
"Slope Arms," "Fix Bayonets," then "Present" they fairly put
    you through it.
And as you stagger to your hut, the Sergeant shouts "Jump to it"

There's another kind of drill, especially invented for the Army,
I think they call it Swedish, and it nearly drives you barmy ;
This blinking drill it does you good, it makes your bones so tender,
You can coil yourself up like a snake and crawl beneath the fender.

With tunics, boots and putties off, you quickly get the habit,
You gallop up and down the hills just like a blooming rabbit,
"Heads Backward Bend," "Arms Upward Stretch," "Heels
    Raise," then "Ranks Change Places,"
And later on they make you put your kneecaps where your face is

Now when this War is over and we've captured Kaiser Billy,
To shoot him would be merciful and absolutely silly,
Just send him down to our little lot, among the rats and clay,
And I'll bet it won't be long before he droops and fades away

  BUT WE'RE STILL "MERRY AND BRIGHT."

From _Cissie_
To _Dad_

7th Battalion was 20-year-old Edgar Ernest Gray, who hailed from the Rows in Great Yarmouth and was a fish hawker by trade. He joined up in August 1914 and was given the service number 12039.

The hard training meted out by the army was far from enjoyable but the men pulled together, as Robert English noted in a letter:

Initial service was for three years, or until the war was over. An infantryman could expect to be paid 7s a week but a member of the Household Cavalry was paid 12s 3d. A sapper could expect to be paid up to 22s 2d depending on specialisation.

I cannot fail to notice the way the fellows who came up at the same time as myself and even later, have come disciplined. In a true British way they grumble terribly at everything which they consider curtailing their liberty, or which involves extra energy on their part. Yet they always do it. As an example, last Thursday we had a little march over 14 miles in full service marching order. Old hands declare they never had such a stiff one because the rests were so limited. Yet out of over 500 men only 5 fell out. But the 'grousing'! It was awful! I do not mean this to show that there is dissatisfaction in the Regiment but as an example of how the average Britisher loves to grumble and yet performs. I think it is amusing.

The Threat of Invasion

It was not just the Western Front and other theatres of war that alarmed the authorities, however, and the threat of an invasion along the east coast of Great Britain was also a major cause for concern. It is not surprising, therefore, that the government were quick to pass an act to prepare for the possibility of an invasion. The Defence of the Realm Act (DORA) was passed by the House of Commons on 8 August 1914 and enabled the government to imprison individuals without trial and suppress those who spoke out against the war. The Act gave the British Government powers to commandeer any resource necessary to further the war efforts and also allowed them to impose restrictions on the press while simultaneously stipulating that anything published which could aid the enemy was regarded as an offence.

This had wide implications for the press of the time, which was apt to report the progress of the war, good or bad. Censorship was high on the agenda and the War Office Press Bureau, initially headed by Frederick Edwin Smith, was established to decide what would be censored and what could be reported.

Kitchener appointed an official war correspondent, Colonel Ernest Swinton, who became the British Army's approved journalist on the Western Front. As the war progressed this changed and other correspondents were allowed to report the war but they too had to accept that the authorities could control what they wrote.

One of the biggest considerations of DORA was what to do if an invasion did happen, how the civilian population would have to act and who would assist the military in protecting and controlling their movements. Norfolk formed part of the Eastern Command where it came under the 9th Grouped Regimental District. As well as the Norfolk regiment there was a cavalry barracks which was home to the 12th (Prince of Wales's Royal) Lancers. These men were part of 5th Cavalry Brigade and there were detachments of Royal Engineers and Army Service Corps at Norwich with a depot for the Royal Garrison Artillery at Great Yarmouth. But by September 1914, the 12/Lancers were in France and questions were raised as to how the county might be defended.

An early example of what was discussed can be seen in the minutes of the Aylsham Police District No. 2 which held a meeting on 7 December 1914 in the Town Hall. Part of the debate dealt with whether a 'Volunteer Corps' should be formed and whether they should be drilled and armed. This sort of question stemmed from the fact that other districts were raising what became known as the Volunteer Training Corps, including Norwich which raised the 1st (City of Norwich) Battalion Norfolk Volunteers. Other areas raised detachments and they were used by both the War Office and the Admiralty for home defence. However, Aylsham District decided not to follow suit. The minutes noted, '… "Special Constables" would be more of a suitable term than "Volunteers".' The committee then decided that the drill was, '… unnecessary as no doubt the

Defence of the Realm invasion orders for the Great Eastern Railway. (William Marriott Museum)

only work they would be called upon to do would be to guard bridges etc, and as regards arms, the ordinary shot gun would be as good as anything for the purpose.' During the next meeting, held on 21 December 1914 and attended by the Chief Constable of Norfolk County, Major Egbert Napier, it was decided that only Special Constables would be used in the Aylsham District.

The contribution made by men who joined up as Special Constables was far from insignificant. Norwich City Police initially swore in 680 men as Specials in 1914 and would eventually recruit 760 to help with the local war effort. Their duties included guarding bridges as well as gas and electrical works. Some were armed but most only carried a truncheon, and uniforms were non-existent until 1916. One man who joined these ranks was Frederick Eaton, who was told by his doctor that he would not be eligible for military service. He notes that the duties of a 'Special' were not easy: 'As the war proceeded the "Specials" duties became more and more arduous and the younger fit men were gathered in to serve their country by donning khaki.'

Part of the duties for both Specials and regular police officers was enforcing the Aliens Act of 1914, whereby foreign nationals had to register with the police while steps were taken to enable their deportation and restrict where they could live. In response to the perceived threat of enemy spies, Egbert Napier instructed his men to work undercover hunting for enemy agents, even sending a naturalised German-speaking officer out to test the resolve of the defences put in place. William Le Queux, who wrote of spies at large in England in 1915, mentioned this work and revealed that Norfolk's local population were tested by an officer of Russian descent who could speak fluent German!

Within a fortnight this shrewd officer returned to me with a hopeless story. Wherever he went the Coastguard refused to tell him anything, or any of their suspicions, as they said they were sworn to secrecy, while the superin-tendents and inspectors of the Norfolk Constabulary, with few exceptions, even though he bore proper credentials signed by the Chief Constable himself, actually refused to give him any assistance or information whatsoever!

Edith Cavell

Perhaps one of the most successful pieces of propaganda utilised during the Great War was linked to the fate of a woman who had been born and bred in Norfolk. Edith Cavell, a nurse who came from Swardeston, had been training student nurses at the L'Ecole Belge d'Infirmières Diplômées in Brussels and was there when war was declared. Edith continued to treat wounded soldiers when Brussels fell and, as a result of

Edith Cavell, Norfolk heroine, executed by the Germans on 12 October 1915. (Author's collection)

49

In total, 33,000 men would serve overseas in the Norfolk Regiment. Three service battalions were raised in the first few weeks of the war – 22 August 1914 (7th Battalion), 4 September 1914 (8th Battalion) and 9 September 1914 (9th Battalion) – and between them the three battalions initially raised around 3,100 men.

the rapid retreat of the BEF, many British soldiers became trapped behind enemy lines. It is estimated that Edith helped at least five men from the 1/Norfolks to escape after Mons. This included Charlie Scott, who had been seriously wounded and was carefully hidden by a succession of Belgian families. He eventually ended up in Edith's care but, with the Germans conducting house searches for escapees, nowhere was safe. One night, when the German soldiers were approaching nearby houses, Edith told him, 'I may be in trouble and if so you will have to get up, and I shall have to hide you.' He was hidden in a barrel full of apples and luckily the Germans did not find him. However, two members of the escape cell were eventually arrested and, as a result, Edith was detained and admitted that she had been involved in the harbouring of Allied soldiers. She was sentenced to death along with four others and, despite intervention from America and Spain, this sentence was carried out on 12 October 1915 at the National Rifle Range (the Tir Nationale). A German Lutheran prison chaplain obtained permission for the English chaplain, Stirling Gahan, to visit her on the night before she died. 'We partook of the Holy Communion together, and she received the Gospel message of consolation with all her heart. At the close of the little service I began to repeat the words, "Abide with me," and she joined softly in the end.'

It is during this time that Edith is believed to have said the famous words: 'Standing as I do in view of God and Eternity, I realise that patriotism is not enough, I must have no hatred or bitterness towards anyone.' A witness to her execution – Pastor Le Seur who was the chaplain appointed by the Germans to minister to the prisoners – described the exact moment she was killed, stating, 'Immediately the sharp commands were given, two salvoes crashed at the same time, each of eight men at a distance of six paces, and the two condemned persons sank to the ground without a sound.'

The execution was used as propaganda by the Allies, who acclaimed Nurse Cavell as a martyr and those responsible for her execution as murderous monsters. Her death became a national sensation with the Home Secretary, Sir Edward Grey, noting.

News of the execution of this noble Englishwoman will be received with horror and disgust, not only in the Allied States, but throughout the civilised world. Miss Cavell was not even charged with espionage, and the fact that she had nursed numbers of German soldiers might have been regarded as a complete reason in itself for treating her with leniency.

3

WORK OF WAR

As previously mentioned, the herring fleets of Great Yarmouth and King's Lynn exported a large proportion of their catch. In fact, 85 per cent of it was exported and the largest shipments – with an average of 2.4 million barrels of pickled herring – went to Russia and Germany. By 15 August 1914, the drifters in Great Yarmouth were all berthed and the town was hit especially hard by the fact that its livelihood was effectively closed down overnight. The *EDP* recorded in August 1914:

> From Yarmouth boats there are said to be as many as 35 per cent of the men similarly called up. How far our fleet can prosecute the herring voyage from Yarmouth is very doubtful in view of the Admiralty request that fishing boats be withdrawn from the North Sea.

As a result many owners simply gave their trawlers and drifters over to the Admiralty. This included James Bloomfield, owner of Bloomfields Ltd in Great Yarmouth, who donated his fleet of twenty steam drifters, plus their crews, to the Admiralty.

The fishing trade came to a complete halt when, in November 1914, the German Navy raided Great Yarmouth and laid mines along the coast. Two steam drifters were lost in the aftermath; one from Lowestoft, the *Fraternal*, and one from Great Yarmouth, the *Copious*. Out of a crew of ten men on the *Copious*, only one man survived.

This provoked further scares that spies were operating in Norfolk. One report suggested that headlights had been used to guide enemy crafts, including Zeppelins, to their targets. An account written by the chief constable of King's Lynn, Inspector Charles Hunt, totally refuted these allegations and states, 'No reports were received from my officers that any car or any person in any car was behaving or doing anything of a suspicious character.' Nevertheless, Major Egbert Napier put his resources to hunting for spies along the Norfolk coastline. 'Official' evidence of this can be found in police officers' pocket notebooks and also in the fact that a number of county constabulary officers were commended for their work, one example being Edward Woodson whose personal record notes that he was, 'Specially commended by the War Office and Home Office for work in connection with the aliens and suspected persons in this County prior to and since the outbreak of war.'

Major Egbert Napier, Chief Constable of the Norfolk County Constabulary, is in the centre of this photograph. (Norfolk Constabulary Historical Collection)

Inspector Carter of Holt Division also assisted the military authorities in the investigation and detention of alleged spies. In June 1916 he detained a Mr Cox and a Miss Andrews for sketching on the seafront at Sheringham where they had 'entirely forgot there was any regulations', and he also investigated a man called 'Osbourne' (later corrected to 'Osborne') who had been:

> ... asking questions respecting military matters from soldiers. Saw Cpl Ernest Evans 43rd Prov Battn TF at Weybourne re same who stated that about 10.30 a.m. on Wednesday 17th May he was playing billiards in Osbourne's house with Rifleman Bentwhistle of the Battn. Osbourne went into the room and asked how many troops camp into Weybourne and joined his Regt, and also asked the correct number of troops now at the camp.

Inspector Carter located an 'Arthur Richard Osborne of Abby Farm House at Weybourne' and interviewed him about the allegations made by the 'Military Authorities'. Osborne stated that, 'I was ignorant of what a Battalion or Company was. I do not recollect saying anything to the troops in my house or anything respecting military matters.'

Carter's notes on the matter suggest that the case was dismissed as the result of a misunderstanding, but Le Queux's book, *German Spies In England: An Exposure*, seems to imply that there may have been other cases which were not so innocent in nature. He writes that, 'By Major Napier's untiring efforts a very large area has been cleared, more especially from Cromer along by Sheringham, Weybourne, a particularly vulnerable point, and from Cley-next-the-Sea to Wells and King's Lynn.'

In addition to the early allegations made by Henry Upcher against his local hotel manager, a little-known story of spying accused Sir Edgar Speyer – who often stayed at the Sea Marg in Overstrand – of acting for the enemy. Speyer was a close friend of Prime Minister Herbert Henry Asquith and had been appointed privy counsellor in 1909, but he was suspected of treachery on account of his German origins and the

*The Sea Marg
in Overstrand
where suspected
spy Sir Edgar
Speyer often stayed.
(Author's collection)*

business links he had maintained with his birthplace (including his position as a partner in a bank in Frankfurt). Furthermore, his brother James, who was living in America, was actively pro-German. Following the German seaborne raids on Great Yarmouth and other coastal towns, Speyer was accused of signalling German U-Boats from Sea Marg. He was also suspected of using his position in the government to pass on naval secrets.

By September 1914, Speyer had, in fact, cut all business ties with Germany, but, amid the anti-German feelings spreading across the country, this was not enough to prevent him from becoming a figure of hate and ridicule. When the press added fuel to these prejudices he was forced to resign from the Poplar Hospital Board, he had to remove his children from their school and his wife Leonora was ostracised. This led Speyer to write to Asquith on 17 May 1915, stating that:

> For the last nine months I have kept silence and treated with disdain the charges of disloyalty and suggestions of treachery made against me in the Press and elsewhere. But I can keep silence no longer, for these charges and suggestion have now been repeated by public men who have not scrupled to use their position to inflame the overstrained feelings of the people.

The main source of income for Norfolk was farming and it produced wheat and other cereals, fruit and cider, turnips, mangold-wurtzel, flax and seeds as well as breeding horses, oxen, sheep, pigs, rabbits, turkeys and game. In 1910, Norwich held the most important markets for corn and cattle in England.

The Red Cross Hospital in Dereham. (Bishop Bonner's Museum)

Although he received support from Asquith, Speyer continued to be hounded. Later that month he resigned from the Underground Electric Railways Co. of London – the forerunner of the London Underground – and, along with his family, he left for America.

Women of Norfolk

Norfolk's women soon found themselves taking up all sorts of employment now that their men had gone off to fight. By 1915 it was very much apparent that there was a shortage of workers, with many having enlisted and now serving in the army or navy. Later on, conscription would produce further shortages of men and it was recognised that there was a willing pool of women who were all

RED CROSS HOSPITAL, EAST DEREHAM.

too keen to fill these gaps. Therefore, women took on many previously male-orientated roles and began to work in the production of munitions, engine driving or delivering the post. A number worked on the land, becoming dairy farmers or joining the Women's Forage Corps, and many women from Norfolk would find themselves working in other parts of the country helping to support the war effort.

"How can we play 'husbands and wives' when we're both girls?"
"Women are doing all the men's jobs nowadays!"

'Doing Their Bit': a postcard looking at the changing roles of women during the war. (Courtesy of Mike and Muriel Fuller)

Another of the many roles that women were recruited into when war broke out was the Red Cross Voluntary Aid Detachments (VADs), formed in 1909 by the War Office under the supervision of the Red Cross. VADs were trained in first aid and nursing, with county branches springing up all over the country. Volunteers performed general nursing duties and administered first aid, drove ambulances, performed clerical duties and worked in hospital kitchens.

Once suitable houses were found, these hospitals had to be staffed, funded and furnished. Dereham Hospital was founded by the Revd McNaughton-Jones, who offered the vicarage in St Withburga Lane to the VAD and acted as the commandant there. It was estimated that £6 per week would be needed to run the hospital so, by 7 November, a 'Penny Fund' was set up which managed to generate £48 17s 6d per annum. People donated between 1d and 6d each week, which was collected in a number

Dereham Red Cross Hospital. The nurse sitting centrally, with the cross on her apron, is Miss Oldham from Dereham. (Bishop Bonner's Museum)

of ways, including at church services or through door-to-door collection. In total, £115 was raised this way. This hospital employed fifty women, with Miss Latham – a nursing sister from Shoreditch Hospital – as matron, and Miss Leslie from King's College Hospital assisting her.

'*Convoy-Tonight', a sketch depicting the preparation made for wounded at the Norfolk War Hospital. (Norfolk Records Office)*

The hospital opened its doors on 16 November 1914 and its first admissions came in March 1915 in the form of nine English soldiers and one Belgian soldier. They were cared for by two local doctors, Dr Howlett and Dr Duigan, and on 20 March the hospital admitted another sixteen patients. In May 1915 an annex was created, followed by a reading room and another annex in July 1915 to help accommodate what had now risen to thirty-nine patients. Later on, a 'Friends of the Hospital' group was formed, providing gifts and organising fundraising events. Dereham Hospital grew in capacity to eventually hold a total of seventy beds and, during the course of the war, 2,067 patients were treated there. The hospital eventually closed its doors on 5 April 1919.

The type of treatment given to soldiers in these hospitals can be seen in a letter written by Lieutenant Phillip Hewetson. Hewetson had suffered a leg wound at Loos while serving with the 1st Battalion Loyal North Lancashire Regiment and upon returning to home for treatment he wrote that:

> Of course it was dreadfully septic, but by draining it, fomenting it and bathing it, it has now become clean and the bruises and swelling are going fast. The first day I had a dry dressing on it, a great advance. The nurse says by next Wednesday or Thursday the flesh ought to have grown and closed up the hole and then skin will start to grow over it.

Many of the men who passed through these hospitals took the time to write to their carers once they had recovered. In a letter to Margaret Amherst of Tofts Hall VAD dated 30 March 1916, Pioneer 115137 William Jennings of the 3rd Provisional Company Royal Engineers noted, 'I often wonder how you are getting on at Buckenham and think of the grand time I had there, I expect you have got all fresh patients now Dear Matron …'

For those who worked in these hospitals, it was a far from restful time. Ruth Hewetson, Phillip Hewetson's sister, worked as a VAD and, during the heavy fighting in March 1918, she noted, 'The hospital is crammed, 2–3 new wards opened and today men lying out on the grass waiting for beds! Nursing staff have been recalled from leave and now number over 100 …' Ruth also noted that her hospital was treating German prisoners of war, 'Then of course all German prisoners must add to the M.O.'s work hugely, I know some sisters are allowed in for dressings, there are some 200 of them some awfully bad (one with both legs off I heard, another '0' arms).'

James Neville, who had served with the 2/Ox & Bucks from December 1916 onwards, was evacuated on 29 March 1918 and noted this about his experiences of nurses working close to the front line:

The nursing staff hardly had time to look at the labels and anybody who could move a muscle was immediately evacuated to the base. High pressure hardly described such superhuman efforts and yet the sisters and the nurses remained unflurried and cool and just worked on quietly, quickly and efficiently.

In 1912, records from Part IV of the Merchant Shipping Act 1894 for Norfolk's herring fleet showed that King's Lynn had 167 ships of 1,465 tonnage, employing 383 hands, and Great Yarmouth had 442 ships of 7,552, employing 2,451 hands, thereby producing one-fifth of the entire take of the kingdom.

The care system stretched right back to the front, where men were initially treated by unit stretcher-bearers who would have taken the wounded to receive treatment from the Battalion's Medical Officer (MO) at a Regimental Aid Post (RAP). But a RAP could only provide basic services and injured soldiers would have been graded there before being sent to an Advanced Dressing Station (ADS). The brigade's field ambulances operated these and here a soldier would have received further treatment before being moved up the line to a Casualty Clearing Station (CCS). The CCS was the first type of medical facility that could deal with all serious medical cases and was designed to stabilise the wounded until they could be evacuated to hospitals either in France or England.

Although there is no evidence of Norfolk women being killed in action overseas, at least three women from Norfolk now lie in cemeteries in France. These are: Assistant Administrator Anna Marjorie Whall from North Barsham, who died at No. 2 General Hospital at Le Havre; Worker Susannah 'Annie' Hall from Reedham; and Worker Mary Maria Matthews from Buxton. All of them served in the Queen Mary's Army Auxiliary Corps and records show that all of them died from influenza.

By 1918, forty-four VAD hospitals were still active in Norfolk and an interesting newspaper article, printed in the *EDP* on 9 March 1918, made a number of observations on what Norfolk had contributed to the VAD effort in the Great War. Part of the proceedings saw the Countess of

Leicestershire noting, 'Norfolk stood second to none in its work and reputation.' She had received a letter from Sir Arthur Stanley, chairman of the Joint War Committee of the British Red Cross Society and the Order of St John, asking her to thank Norfolk members for the splendid work they have done and adding, 'We have received large sums of money from Norfolk; and I know, from what you have told me, that the recruiting for the V.A.D. has been better in that county than in any other.' But there was also a drive to recruit more as it was noted that, 'The society wanted more members of every kind – cooks, clerks, storekeepers, short-hand writers and typists, ward maids, house members and waitresses.'

The Revd Major G.H. Thompson also spoke, saying that, 'There was every reason to be satisfied with the great work that had been done during the past year by the Norfolk Branch of the Red Cross.' By 1918 it was noted in the *EDP* that there were, 'No fewer than 124 Norfolk girls … working in all parts of the world.' This included Monimia Gwen Snelling from Norwich, whom William Hewetson mentioned in the Wroxham parish magazine, recording that, 'Miss Snelling, after three years' service in England, in December last went to Egypt, and now is with her hospital at Salonica, and there, she says, she really feels on active service.'

In 1916 the minimum wage for skilled workers was up to 30s a week with a 1–2s war bonus for workers over 21 years. But in 1917 it was noted by the local unions that certain firms in Norwich were still paying their workers below the minimum wage.

Other roles taken on by women included working in munitions and a great number, including Victoria Cole from Itteringham, signed up to work at the Harwich Munitions Factory. During the Great War it is estimated that over 2 million women took up work which had previously been left to men. Mrs Millicent Fawcett, the president of the National Union of Women's Suffrage Societies, noted, 'The war revolutionised the industrial position of women, it found them serfs and left them free.' But this new type of work was not without its hazards. Gracia Margaret Bolton from Beeston, who went off to work at No. 6 Shell Filling Factory at Chilwell in Nottinghamshire, would tragically die at the

age of 20 when, on 1 July 1918 at 7.10 p.m., an explosion ripped through the factory. Out of 134 who died, Gracia was one of 102 workers whose remains were unidentifiable. An investigation into the accident found that almost 8 tons of explosive had gone up without warning. She is now laid to rest in a mass grave in Attenborough churchyard.

Victoria Cole, a munitions worker at Harwich, appears here, standing on the extreme left of the second row. (Courtesy of Nathan Waring)

Perhaps the main area of employment for women, especially from 1916 onwards, was farming and women worked extremely hard to prove themselves in this sector. Many employers were impressed by their efforts and certainly Sculthorpe-born Mary Alcock's manager wrote, '… I do not think I can sing their praises too much as a land worker, for she turned out in all weathers and by her manner and conversation put heart into the younger girls.'

Local unions tackled numerous issues such as pay and conditions for war workers. For instance, the local branch of the Electrical Trades Union ensured that its members on active service had their contributions paid by the National Benevolent Fund, thereby ensuring that they were entitled to full benefits once demobilised.

Miss Burton Fanning presenting a Women's Land Army armband to a young girl on Mr J. Thistleton Smith's farm at West Barsham. (Gressinghall Museum)

Victoria Cole's munitions worker identity permit. (Courtesy of Nathan Waring)

By 20 February 1917, however, the Norfolk Women's Agricultural Committee (NWAC) recognised that there was a shortage of women working for the Women's Land Army and Mrs Frances Burton canvassed the county in an effort to revise village registers; adding fresh names or crossing off those who did not keep their promises to work. Mrs Burton wrote to say, 'Should sufficient local women's labour not be available in your village, would you please find out from the farmers if they would be willing to employ whole-time women from elsewhere.'

Suggestions were also made to make representation to the Education Committee to continue Winter School Hours through the summer (so that women could continue to work around school hours), although there is no evidence that this came to fruition. Matters were taken seriously and, on 8 January 1916, the very first course was run for Norfolk women at Chelmsford Agricultural College, teaching twelve girls how to milk cows. The course lasted four weeks and was funded by the Education Committee, with those women who took part being paid £1 12*d* per week for this arduous work. A letter was sent to all members of the NWAC to choose suitable girls for future courses and a speech about the importance of giving vocational training to women was held locally. It concluded by stating: 'And so the new vision is part of the progress – let each one of us prove ourselves – each one forming a centre of help and influence in the progress of women's work that the Women of Britain go forward in national affairs, on education, moral and political lines.'

The Women's Land Army

The Women's Land Army was formed to recruit women aged between 16 and 60 who were willing to work in their parish or neighbourhood or who could, at their own request, work in other parts of the country. Norfolk's women were recruited by the Norfolk Ladies' Committee (NLC), the president of which was the Countess of Leicester, Alice Emily Coke.

Their objectives were listed in a letter to the NLC in August 1916 and they were:

1. To bring the need for all Women to undertake work.
2. To organise women labour & increase the role of women workers so that an organised band of women workers shall be obtained for each parish.
3. To educate women & girls in dairy work, gardening, light farm work, fruit farming, fruit picking, poultry farming etc.
4. To economise in the home.

For instance, evidence from the parish of Brampton shows that nine women initially applied to work on the land. Of these nine, their experience of farm work was mixed. One woman had done some gardening at home, four had no experience of any type of agricultural work, one had weeded for a farmer and two had picked fruit and weeded for a farmer. In all, ten women from Brampton gained the coveted Women's Land Army armlets and cards in 1916.

The service of all such women was greatly appreciated. On 28 February 1919, Lord and Lady Suffield presided over a ceremony at Church House in Dereham to honour their district and spoke on the topic of the Women's Land Army. The *EDP* noted that:

Lord Suffield spoke in the highest praise of the magnificent service they had rendered the country. Although the good service badges he was presenting to them were of no intrinsic value, they possessed a value of their own in so far as they represented a permanent record of the Land Workers' phase in the Great War.

Women's Land Army girls chopping out mangolds. This photo was taken on Mr J. Thistleton Smith's farm at West Barsham. (Gressinghall Museum)

Olive Edis, official war photographer for the National War Museum. (Cromer Museum, Norfolk Museums Service)

And what about Norfolk's official 'first' female war photographer? This was Olive Edis, who had a studio in Church Street in Sheringham. In 1918 she travelled to the Western Front, where she was to photograph the work of the women's services in France. The images were commissioned by the National War Museum but Olive was also able to photograph other subjects, such as Marshall Ferdinand Foch and General Weygand of the French Army, as well as battlefield subjects such as destroyed tanks and the war graves around the Ypres Salient. The photos she took of the war work carried out by women around the Western Front are an amazing testament to the changing role of women within society.

German prisoners were also put to work on the land. By June 1917 there were around eighty prisoners at Narborough and in 1918 a further forty-two were accommodated in the stables at Houghton Hall with fifty at Gressinghall Workhouse. There were also detachments around Dereham and eventually many of these men were put to work digging out drainage ditches around rivers such as the Yare and the Waveney.

A photograph taken by Olive Edis of a destroyed British tank around the Ypres Salient. (Cromer Museum, Norfolk Museums Service)

Wartime Industry

One of the lesser-known industries to come out of Norfolk was the production of acetone, which was an essential solvent used to make cordite. Acetone came from distilled wood but new processes of manufacture meant that it could also be developed from maize and potatoes, products that were mostly imported from America. However, as the U-boat war in the North Atlantic intensified, there was a very real fear that supplies would diminish. Experiments to find alternative sources discovered that acetone could also be derived from the horse chestnut, i.e the conker! The Synthetic Products Company at King's Lynn, which had been producing acetone from potatoes since 1915, was converted to take on the task of producing acetone from conkers and the Ministry of Munitions put out a statement which appeared in *The Times* on 26 July 1917: '… chestnut seeds, not the green husks, are required by the Government for the Ministry of Munitions. The nuts will replace cereals which have been necessary for the production of an article of great importance in the prosecution of the War.'

Schoolchildren and Scouts were encouraged to collect chestnuts for this cause but only 3,000 tins reached the King's Lynn plant, while transport difficulties led to much of this harvest rotting at railways stations across the country. The real reason for the collection remained a secret, even though questions were asked in Parliament and in the papers. The process was begun in April 1918 but horse chestnuts were eventually found to be of poor quality for this type of process and the production was stopped in July 1918.

A good example of a local firm adapting to the war is provided by the general manufacturing firm, Boulton & Paul Ltd. As the war progressed they assisted the war effort in various ways, including building a naval hospital, a prisoner-of-war camp, hangars in England, hospitals in France and warehouses in Mesopotamia. Departments were adapted to make field kitchens and produce electric lighting,

In April 1918 the Norfolk District Wages Committee passed a recommendation to the Agricultural Board, who agreed to pay women the minimum rate of 5*d* per hour with overtime being paid at 9*d*. At that time women were working up to fifty-four hours per week, including over six hours on Saturdays!

and then in 1915 their role changed considerably when they were asked to make aircraft in partnership with Howes & Sons. As a result, the first prototype FE2B flew from the airfield at the Cavalry Drill Ground on Mousehold Heath in 1915. At its height Boulton & Paul made twenty-eight Sopwith Camels a week and constructed a total of 2,500 military aircraft during the course of the war. They were helped by another company who had to adapt to making aircraft parts – Trevor Page & Co., who usually made furniture, produced propellers for aircraft at their factory in Norwich. By 1917, Boulton & Paul were beginning to develop their own aircraft prototypes under the guidance of their chief engineer, John Dudley North. As *Flight Magazine* revealed in 1922:

> Others followed, and before many months the aircraft department of Boulton and Paul had assumed large proportions. Other types of machines were built, notably a very great number of Sopwiths, and ultimately almost the whole of the extensive works in Norwich, as well as the new works built at Mousehold, were busy turning out aircraft.

This eventually saw the employment of some 2,000 people at the Rose Lane Works including a number of women. Records from the company also mention the expansion of another firm, Laurence Scott & Co., who employed over 500 people by October 1914. Both firms assisted the Admiralty in building new shops to make 3- and 5-inch shells at a rate of 250 shells per day for the duration of the war. However, in relation to men and women working together, not everything ran smoothly. Mr Lubbock of the Electrical Trades Union noted in a letter dated 2 January 1917 that,

A peacock made by a German prisoner of war whilst working around Dereham. (Gressinghall Museum)

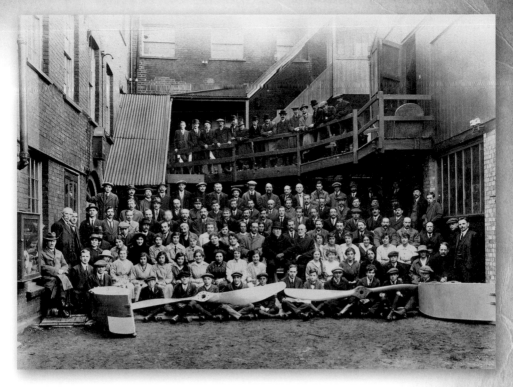

Workers from Trevor Page & Co. during the First World War. (Picture Norfolk)

'A deputation from the Winding Department approached the Works Manager and a question relating to the female workers in that Dept.' It appeared that the women were accused of '… trying to dictate to the Works Manager.' It is not known how this complaint was dealt with but no further deputations came forward after this!

Raising Funds

As the conflict progressed, money constantly needed to be raised for the war effort. From Monday, 1 April 1918, 'Norwich Tank Week' was held in an effort to raise war bonds, with a tank displayed outside the Guildhall. The *EDP* reported that the most memorable part of the week was arranged by the newly formed National Union of Women Workers.

The Women's Land Army was formed in February 1917 and in total 23,000 women volunteered, having to pass a strict selection process before entering employment. The Land Army was divided into three main sections: agricultural, forestry and animal feeding. It was disbanded in December 1919.

'There were units of munition girls in uniform, including a large party from Norwich Components and parties also representing women railway workers, Carrow Works, the Women's Land Army, the Women's Co-Operative Guild, Milk Girls and women and girls employed in printing and allied trades.' The article revealed that the female workers of J. & J. Colman alone had

Norwich Tank Week, April 1918. (Norfolk Constabulary Historical Collection)

Gladys Cobb, who served in Queen Mary's Army Auxiliary Corp, is seen sitting on the right of the sergeant. (Courtesy of Nick Cobb)

raised £1,219 4s 6d. The final day of Tank Week saw the *EDP* report that, 'The success of the week is already assured; but we are not content with a measure of success below a million; and we trust that today's final effort will achieve it.'

And meet it they did. A final ceremony was held and further funds were donated, including two cheques from Norwich City Police whereby the chief constable, John Henry Dain, presented the Lord Mayor, Richard Jewson, with a total of £50,000 raised through private donations from police officers and their families. In total a staggering £1,057,382 was raised for the war effort.

During the war there were sixty-four women's detachments in Norfolk, of which fifty-one were mobilised. In total, 124 women from Norfolk served in the VAD overseas.

4

NEWS FROM THE FRONT LINE

Phillip Hewetson landed in France on 4 June 1915 and wrote to his parents on 29 August 1915 to say: 'I have never been able to appreciate what the feelings of the tramp with no roof to his head are so well as I have the last 24 hours.' He was talking about his experiences in the trenches and this was now the reality for all those who were serving on the Western Front. Both sides were at a stalemate and occupied a trench system that spanned from the Belgian coast to the Swiss border. Hewetson went on to describe the trenches themselves:

They are about 2 feet wide and 7 to 8 feet deep so unless a lucky shell drops right into one you are quite safe. The trenches our men are in are about 5 or 6 feet deep, they are made in two levels, one to walk along and a platform about 1 ft high and 1 ft broad to stand on to fire. They are about 3 ft wide. Thus you fire over a parapet not through a loophole.

Phillip Hewetson served in the Loyal North Lancashire Regiment. (Norfolk Records Office)

Even though the two sides were in stalemate, there was an air of optimism. Private Upton, serving in the 2/South Staffords, wrote to Lady Amhurst: 'France is a lovely country but it has been terribly knocked about since the war, but we all live and hope that the time is not far distant when we shall once more be in dear old England and the war brought to a victorious finish …'

But the Western Front was a dangerous place to be and Frederick Cubitt, who served with the Army Service Corps, experienced one such hazard when he was subjected to an artillery strike near Poperinghe, 'I shouted out, "Get down!" and Bloomfield shouted out, "It's too late!" and next minute we found ourselves in the ditch by the side of the road with shell, bricks and shrapnel flying over the top of us.'

The Great War was, above all else, an artillery war and Phillip Hewetson also gave his parents an insight into the realities of this:

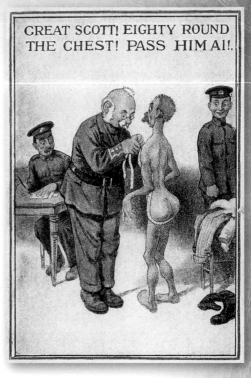

GREAT SCOTT! EIGHTY ROUND THE CHEST! PASS HIM AI!.

The lighter side of enlistment, as seen in 1918. (Courtesy of Mike and Muriel Fuller)

What both sides trouble each other most with are trench mortars. The best of these is that you can see them coming – looking like a black oblong sausage about 2 feet long and 5 or 6 inches in diameter. They are fired at a range varying from one to three 100 hundred [*sic*] and go up to a height of 50–100 feet in order to get them to fall into the trench.

Attempts were made to break the deadlock and Captain Neville-Rolfe, now serving with the 2/8th Gurkha Rifles, saw action at the Battle of Neuve Chappelle (a village positioned around flat farmland surrounded by drainage ditches between Bethune and Armentières) on 10 March 1915. It was initially successful but Arthur Neville-Rolfe noted that it was hampered by the lack of artillery shells:

75

Gun ammunition had been so tightly rationed when I was out in 1914 that a twenty-minute preliminary bombardment sounded quite phenomenal. We had started the war with very inadequate supplies of gun ammunition, and when trench warfare developed the emphasis was all on H.E. An H.E. bombardment is most impressive but I doubt whether it is as good as shrapnel for wire cutting. Be that as it may much of the German wire was uncut that day.

The Allied high command also faced a setback to their plans when the Germans struck at Ypres on 22 April, launching the first gas attacks of the war. The 1/Norfolks were positioned around Hill 60 at this time and the regimental history records that: 'During the early part of May the 1st Norfolk remained in the same trenches till, after suffering seventy-five casualties from gas on the 5th, they were relieved on the 6th.'

William England was killed in action at Ypres on 27 May 1915. (Courtesy of Les Fisher)

Casualties for this period include Adjutant Captain William C.K. Megaw, killed on 31 March, and William England, who was in the line at Verbrande Molen near Hill 60 on 27 May.

The three service battalions landed in France between May and August 1915. The 7/Norfolks initially served to the south of Ypres around Ploegsteert and the other two battalions found themselves on the Somme. One man who would land in France at this time would be Edgar Gray, who arrived with the 7/Norfolks on 30 May 1915. But the first major action fought by the Norfolk Regiment in 1915 would be carried out by a TF battalion who took part in the ill-fated campaign in the Dardanelles, which was designed to bring victory in a campaign operating away from the Western Front.

The 5/Norfolks, serving in the 163rd Brigade of the 54th (East Anglian) Division, landed at Suvla Bay on 12 August and, two days after their arrival, were ordered to attack the Turkish lines with the rest of the brigade and clear the enemy from the village of Kuchuk Anafarta Ova. Sergeant T. Jakeman of C Company recalled that they had advanced no further than 50 yards when, 'From the hills on the right belched forth a terrific cannonade of shrapnel; from the left came hail like machine gun and rifle fire; and bullets came from machine guns and rifles in front.'

Casualties were incurred almost immediately, forcing the battalion to rush the enemy in bursts while their numbers dwindled as more and more fell as a result of the fierce bombardment and heat exhaustion. Smaller groups managed to reach a small vineyard and a cluster of small cottages, and it was at this point that the surviving officers managed to take stock of what had happened, leading the survivors back to friendly lines when it became dark. The battalion's war diary was short and to the point: '163rd Brigade made a frontal attack on strong Turkish position. 5th NFKs on right met a strong opposition and suffered heavily and lost 22 officers and about 350 men.'

George Ormiston talked about his experience of going over the top with the 1/Warwickshire Yeomanry at Chocolate Hill and Hill 112 in Gallipoli:

No doubt by now you know some of the boys have gone under. We had a nasty shelling on the 21st August in fact we never realised what was awaiting us although our officers must have known and I considered it a plucky movement of theirs. I managed to scrape through alright but I thought my number was up once or twice. I got a small flesh wound on my shins by a piece of shrapnel but nothing to speak of.

The fighting at Gallipoli – designed to draw enemy forces away from critical areas along the Western and Eastern fronts – would sadly never produce the effect that its commanders had hoped for. It was viewed by many to be an ill-advised campaign and a great number of Allied forces died as a result of disease in addition to the fierce Turkish onslaughts.

We can never know the total number of Norfolk men who were wounded during the war, but 2,219 men were invalided out of the army and awarded a Silver War Badge as a result of wounds, illness or the fact that they were no longer fit to serve.

Another engagement to take place towards the end of 1915 was the Battle of Loos, fought between September and October of that year, and it was here that both the 7 and 9/Norfolk would see action. This conflict took place on ground that is extremely flat and, at the time, was an important mining area. It was studded with pitheads and slag heaps known as *crassiers* and *fosses*; these geographical features were used by both sides as observation points and defensive positions.

But the next major battle, considered to be the 'Big Push' for 1916, would be fought over the chalky soil of the Somme region in France. It would be a baptism of fire for the three Norfolk Royal Engineer Field Companies of the 34th Division. The strategy of this battle would see British and French artillery continually assaulting the Germans in an effort to destroy the German barbed wire and defences. Lieutenant Sidney Smith of the 7/Norfolks noted this in the build-up to the battle:

> I am now about 28 miles from the firing line and can hear the roar of cannon. French and British airships are always about, it's awful that wherever you go you see camp after camp full of troops, but I think they will all be wanted and practically every man in England to end the war.

Whilst waiting for zero-hour, Herbert Cooper of the 8/Norfollks described the bombardment that would eventually last for seven days:

> You must excuse paper and bad writing as we are in the midst of a terrific bombardment, no doubt it's heaven in Blighty. By now what's taking place all along the line looks impossible for anything to live through this lot but no doubt some of us will see it to the end if we are lucky.

Sadly, for many of the troops attacking, the hopes that Herbert laid out in his letter would prove to be unfounded. The intense bombardment failed to destroy the German bunkers deep underground and would, in fact, prove largely ineffective. The terrible loss of life that followed is reflected in the fate of the Norfolk troops present and the 34th Division in particular.

On 1 July 1916, the 34th Division advanced on La Boiselle and managed to occupy the massive mine crater called 'Lochnagar' and a defensive position called Scots Redoubt but further advances could not be made. It was here that all three Norfolk field companies were used to support the troops who were occupying these positions. The war diary for the 208th Field Company reveals that: 'Several casualties were sustained and the sections became scattered. About 40 men were collected and remained in our lines under 2nd Lt C.A. Ablett until 2 p.m. when they were utilised by carrying bombs and water to the south mine crater via the tunnels until 9.30 p.m.'

Soldiers Died in the Great War records a total of 6,026 casualties in the Norfolk Regiment. However, the Commonwealth War Graves Commission lists this as 6,282. Chronologically the count per year was 229 (1914), 1,038 (1915), 1,696 (1916), 1,888 (1917) and 1,310 men (1918) killed.

La Boiselle on the Somme in 1917. (Author's collection)

La Boiselle did not fall that day and the 34th Division lost 6,811 men – all killed or wounded between the 1 and 5 July – including eight senior officers. This included Harry Hazel, who had joined up with his friends from Norwich City Police. At Montauban the 8/Norfolks assisted in its capture and witnessed the 8/E Surrey Regiment kicking footballs across no-man's-land. Taking part in this action was Charlie Wells, who came from Coltishall. A letter written to Charlie's sister by his company commander described his death:

> We had to face a very heavy rifle and machine-gun fire, and nearing the front German trench the lines slackened pace slightly. Seeing this Wilfred dashed in front with a bomb in his hand and was immediately shot through the head almost side by side with Soames and Sgt Major Wells.

Leslie Fisher served in the same battalion as war poet Edmund Blunden. (Courtesy of Les Fisher)

There was no let up on the Somme and the battle now became part of a number of continual pushes. All four battalions of the Norfolk Regiment on the Western Front would see action there at places that became synonymous with the Somme: Delville Wood, Longueval, Mouquet Farm, Falfemont Farm, Thiepval, Transloy Ridges, the Ancre Heights and the Schwaben Redoubt. During this terrible fighting a man from Cromer would die serving in the same battalion as war poet Edmund Blunden – Lance Corporal Leslie Fisher is now laid to rest in Mill Road Cemetery built on the Schwaben Redoubt. He died fighting around Stuff Trench. From the Norfolk Regiment alone, 1,127 men fell in the action fought between 1 July and 18 October 1916 and are laid to rest in the cemeteries on the Somme.

Archie Milk from Dereham enlisted in Canada on 7 June 1915 and went on to serve with the 52nd Battalion, Manitoba Regiment. His battalion would also see action on the Somme when they took part in the Battle of Flers Courcelette. The war diary for the 52nd Battalion states:

> Crossing the field up the slope at R.28.d south of Farbeck Green between Sunken Road and Centreway Trench, the Battalion came under intense bombardment of artillery, machine gun and rifle fire, suffering heavy casualties in officers and other ranks. Just before reaching the jumping off trench the O.C. and the Adjutant were both wounded by rifle bullets.

Archie's battalion lost eleven officers and 244 men from other ranks were killed or wounded.

But trench warfare was not just about fighting staged battles. In periods of quiet it was expected that patrols would be mounted. If we return to the events of October 1915 at Gallipoli, an excellent account of one of these patrols can be found in the diary of Captain Geoffrey Barker, who led a group of men into no-man's-land and walked into a Turkish patrol: 'As they were nearly round us we had to retire which we did pretty quick, 3 of the 5 of us tripped over stones and fell over and the Turks came on about 8 yards and I thought they would try to rush us but luckily were afraid and stopped.' Fortunately, Barker and his men got back to their lines unscathed.

The early months of 1917 would see the 8/Norfolks advancing towards the south-east of Miraumont on the Somme and their attack on Hill 130, which took place on 17 February, achieving partial success. At Arras, the 7/Norfolks helped

Archie Milk served in the 52nd Manitoba Regiment. (Bishop Bonners Museum)

carry the day with the capture of over ninety Germans and, moving along the Cambrai Road, the seizure of Maison Rouge.

But one of the largest actions of 1917 occurred in Palestine, where the British had been defending the Suez Canal against the Turks and Arab tribes known as the Senussi. Here the 4 and 5/ Norfolks saw action at the Second Battle of Gaza on 19 April. This encounter, utilising six Australian and British divisions, was fought using Western Front weapons such as gas and tanks. It was doomed to failure. 'We suddenly heard a tremendous rattling noise coming from behind & keeping my head as low as possible I chanced a look behind & saw a tank coming at full speed not a hundred yards behind & firing all her guns which was a fine sight to see.'

The tank was HMLS *Nutty*. Commanded by Second Lieutenant Frank Carr, his efforts to draw the attention of the Turks away from the Australian and British forces were described by the Australian Camel Brigade as 'the finest bit of shooting they had ever seen'. Nevertheless, Carr failed to stop the Turkish counter-attack, the tank was disabled and Carr and his crew were killed or captured.

Both sides, on all fronts of the war, held a certain respect for each other and times of ceasefire were maintained for rituals such as burying the dead or eating meals. Phillip Hewetson wrote that: 'Both sides are very much the same you know, in some ways both English and German must have breakfast etc and also some rest between 4 to 7 every morning after the strain of the night. One German shouted out one morning, "When do you have breakfast, we have ours at 7!"'

Soon after this, the defenders of Tank Redoubt ran out of both ammunition and men. Private Emms described the withdrawal: '… our officer shouted out that we should either have to give in or make a run for it, so we decided to make a dash for it & only one officer & seven men managed to get away.' By the end of this battle, the two Norfolk battalions alone had lost 1,158 officers and men and in total the six divisions had lost 5,917 men.

It was not just enemy action that caused casualties, however, and conditions for everyone serving at the front were hard, with illness taking its toll on the men. Captain Neville-Rolfe became ill in 1917 while serving in Mesopotamia:

… I contracted a very virulent attack of jaundice during the coldest spell of weather that I ever remember in Mesopotamia. I knew that I ought to have gone sick, but I also knew it meant being sent down to Basra, and once there, it might take months to get sent to the front again.

HMLS Nutty
which supported the 5/Norfolks at the 2nd Battle of Gaza. (Author's collection)

The Norfolk Regiment's history records the terrible conditions in the trenches during the winter of 1916/17, '… when the whole group came off duty one hour after daylight they had to turn into a dark, muddy dugout, sodden with wet, caked with mud, and exhausted with cold and exposure, and sleep, if they could, just as they were.'

One man who contracted trench fever during this period was Sapper Thomas Green who was evacuated home. Sadly, like many others who contracted this illness, he died at home and is now laid to rest in Norwich Cemetery.

By February 1917, after the 2/Norfolks recovered from the Siege of Kut, they reformed and became part of the 37th Brigade in the 14th Indian Division. This battalion had suffered terribly while driving the Turks out of Kut before advancing on Baghdad and the German-built Berlin-Baghdad railway. By this time, the war in this theatre was effectively ending and the 2/Norfolks advanced up the right bank of the Diala before the fall of Baghdad in March 1917. Captain Neville-Rolfe made note of the destruction the Turks had left in the city in an effort to build a new road. 'When we arrived the road was in working order though the half demolished houses on each side looked like London in the blitz.'

The war on the Western Front carried on with a sweeping victory at Messines during the summer of 1917. Less well known is the action seen by the 34th Division between 26 August and 11 September, when it took over a section of 3rd Corps ground around the Hargicourt-L'Omignon River sector. Here the division took part in an operation designed to capture part of the Hindenburg Line. On 1 September, another police officer from Norwich, Henry Crisp, was killed

Norfolk pals of the 1st Battalion: Alfred Dunnett and Ernest Denham were killed in action, William Russell was medically discharged and John Williams died of his wounds. The rest survived the war. (Norfolk Records Office)

WEEKLY PRESS. SATURDAY, DECEMBER 2, 1916.

NORFOLK PIONEERS.

Pioneers. — Battalion, Norfolks, with their trench-worn dog Pedro, who is suffering from wounds caused by contact with barbed wire entanglements.
Standing:—E. Denham (Norwich), H. Francis (Shotesham), Lance-Corporal Williams (Yarmouth), W. Russell (Norwich).
H. A. Dunnett (Downham), Sergeant Gilham (Dereham), C. Russell (Lynn), A. B. Dunnett (Cambridge), Pedro, J. Ringer (Gissing).

The original grave marker at Hargicourt for Henry Crisp. (Courtesy of Alan Forsdick)

Records show that 11,895 Norfolk men were killed in action, died of wounds or perished as a result of other circumstances while serving in the army. A total of 783 died serving with the Royal Navy, Royal Marines or the Royal Naval Division and thirty-seven men died serving in the Royal Flying Corps or Royal Air Force.

during the fighting here and a letter from a friend noted, 'Well I thought I'd first write and let you know that I fixed Harry's cross up before I left that place.'

The Third Battle of Ypres was fought between 31 July and 10 November. Here the 8/Norfolks saw action at Glencourse Wood and went over the top on 22 October 1917, supported by elements of the 34th Division on their left, assaulting Requete at Poelcapelle. Prior to this, all three of the field companies of the 34th Division had been utilised to build roads. As the history of the division states, 'A nasty job in the forward area, carried out under the worst weather conditions, and under almost continual shell fire.'

During the advance at Poelcapelle, the field companies operated around Langemarck with the divisional artillery. The engineers lost 100 men and 425 men from the 8/Norfolks now lie in Flanders Fields. Other casualties at the Third Battle of Ypres included Gunners Skipper and Snelling who died on the same day, 12 October. Archie Skipper died in counter battery fire close to Birr Cross Roads and Cornelius Snelling died in 47th CCS, where his death was recorded in a letter:

> I thought I would take the liberty to write to let you know, he was well cared for during the brief time he was here and also I done all he wished, he died peacefully from a shrapnel wound in the chest, hoping you will forgive the liberty I am taking in writing.

Both sides carried out trench raids in order to keep their enemy on their toes or to gather intelligence. At 4.55 p.m. on 14 October 1917, the 7/Norfolks carried out a raid on German trenches near to Monchy-le-Preux. After a sustained bombardment that lasted six hours, a party of the Norfolks entered the German lines and, although the German lines were well defended, the enemy either surrendered or fled. 'Our men could

Gunner Archie Snelling, who died of wounds at 47 Casualty Clearing Station on 12 October 1917.
(Picture Norfolk)

Gunner Cornelius Skipper, killed in action on 12 October 1917 at Birr Cross Roads, Ypres. (293rd siege battery website)

Between 1914 and 1915, 2,062 Norfolk men were killed in action, died of wounds or died while serving in the army. This increased to 2,916 men in 1916, many of whom died while serving in regiments that fought on the Somme between 1 July and 18 November 1916.

not be prevented from killing those that surrendered and it is estimated that at least 200 Germans were killed by the raiders while many dead were found as a result of our bombardment.'

All objectives were met with 'slight' casualties – six officers killed or wounded and sixty-six other ranks killed or wounded. Amongst the wounded was Edgar Gray.

Both the 7 and 9/Norfolks would see action at the Battle of Cambrai, fought between 20 November and 7 December, the first battle to see the mass use of tanks. The 9/Norfolks took part in the assault on the village of Ribecourt, overrunning the enemy tanks and meeting with stiff resistance until their own tanks caught up with them. By 9 a.m., 20 November, the battalion had captured 500 Germans. But success at Cambrai ended in failure when the Germans counter-attacked on 30 November. By this time the 7/Norfolks were in the line at Villers-Guislain and it was here that enemy forces confronted them at 8 a.m. that morning. Although they put up a staunch defence they were overwhelmed with terrible losses, including their commanding officer, Lieutenant Colonel H.L.F.A. Gielgud, and 351 officers and men.

In 1917 the number of deaths rose to 3,817 Norfolk men, mainly due to casualties who fell at Arras, Messines, Third Ypres and Cambrai. The figure for 1918 was 3,080, with casualties mainly being incurred during the German Spring Offensive and in the last 100 days, when the Allies advanced to victory.

Between December 1917 and March 1918 there was a lull as both sides settled in for the winter. Sadly, after three years of serving on the Western Front, the 8/Norfolks were disbanded and its ranks were sent to the 7th and 9th Norfolks or were drafted into other regiments. As noted in the regiment's war diary, this was a sad occasion, with the final entry, dated 20 February 1918, stating: 'It is thus assumed that the 8th (Service) Battalion the Norfolk Regiment ceased to exist from today.'

This battalion stands out on account of their great sacrifice during the war. They saw some of the heaviest fighting on the Western Front and as the Norfolk's history states, 'As for the some 770 of our comrades who will not return, to them is due the greatest of all debts …'

But a lull over the winter did not see an end to the fighting and, by March 1918, Germany was ready to launch its last great offensive of the war. This became known as Kaiserschlacht, the Kaiser's Battle. Both the 7th and 9th Norfolks saw heavy fighting during this time but, as the situation worsened, other units were put into the line including the Norfolk Royal Engineers. The 34th Division, fighting in the Forward Zone near Croisilles, suffered so many casualties that, '… into this trench the 34th Division ordered its pioneers and the three field companies, its last reserves.'

James Neville was able to observe the enemy numbers whilst occupying Dyke Valley overlooking the Albert-Bapaume Road at Le Sars on the old Somme battlefield on 25 March 1918:

> They were well trained and made excellent use of ground and cover, and never exposed themselves unnecessarily. Their first consideration was to manoeuvre the light machine guns forward, to cover the advance of the rest. Through my glasses I picked up a man carrying one of these guns and directed my Lewis gun on him. He never carried that or any other gun again.

34th Division Signals on 6 March 1918 at Gommiecourt. (Courtesy of Gerald Statham)

James Neville, along with the rest of the British and French in this sector, would continually retreat until the German advance was halted to the east of Amiens at Villers-Bretonneux by Australian and British troops on 24 April 1918. By 15 July 1918, James Neville noted, 'Sometimes I feel that there is a faint hope of it being over before the winter. The German soldiers will be so fed up if it isn't.'

James Nevill whilst on active service at Quesnoy in 1917. (Norfolk Records Office)

In many respects he was right and the turning point of the war was coming.

Trench Warfare

Trench warfare was not one continuous push between two armies. Life in the trenches generally meant intense periods of boredom and toil mixed with short periods of action. Battalions would often only spend four days in a row in the front line before being relieved by another battalion from their brigade. This would provide the battalion with a chance to rest up and to recuperate.

A typical day in the front line would start at around dawn with both sides standing to, as this was when the enemy was most likely to launch an attack. The men would man the fire steps and often fired off thousands of rounds of ammunition, which became known as the 'Morning Hate'. This could also be mixed with artillery fire.

Once this was over, life would generally settle and then revolve around getting the men fed, with many using this time to try and relax or catch up on sleep. However, this quiet time could be rudely shattered by stray shells and snipers. Moreover, there were always chores to be done and many would find themselves on work details, ensuring that the trenches were well kept. As dusk fell, another stand to would be ordered and it was after this that hot food could be brought up. The rum ration was also issued at this point.

Once night fell, men could move more freely and parties were often put into no-man's-land to repair the wire or to gather intelligence about the German lines. Occasionally, trench raids were sanctioned and parties would infiltrate the German lines. Although the two sides often tried to maintain a 'live and let live' policy, these raids were still fraught with danger and could lead to retaliation from the enemy.

Men on fatigue duty building a dug-out at Bazetin-le-Petit on the Somme in 1916. (Author's collection)

5

HOME FIRES BURNING

The attacks on Norfolk that took place in November 1914 and January 1915 – by both the German Navy and enemy Zeppelins – were discussed by the Local Emergency Committees which were set up all over the county. These committees acted under the direction of the Central Emergency Committee, with Lord Lieutenant Thomas William Coke acting as chairman and able to liaise with the military authorities. On 31 May 1915, the Aylsham District Chairman sent a telegram to Mr Cheetham of Cawston Manor, stating:

> I sincerely trust you will be able to attend as I particularly want to bring before you the question of the attempts which will undoubtedly be made by the Germans from airships to burn the corn crops before the harvest is cut, and to consider the best possible means of meeting this danger.

This fear probably stems from the fact that both Zeppelins dropped incendiary bombs in fields, an attack on the county that provoked many different reactions. The relevance of these raids were discussed nationally with *The War Illustrated* also wanting to know why they had been launched: 'When considered [alongside] raids on the coast, such as Hartlepool or the recent air raid on the coast of Norfolk, such action again has no military value unless it leads to dispersion of effort from offensive to the defensive.'

Phillip Hewetson, now serving at home with the 3/Loyal North Lancashire Fusiliers, provides us with an insight into what it was like to be in a Zeppelin raid in 1916:

> We had a great night here last night. We got a splendid view twice as the searchlights found them and they showed as plain as anything. They had a nasty time as all the guns strafed them from all round, it was quite a battle!! Shells and bombs bursting, though not so very near here, but tremendously exciting.

Exciting or not, these raids caused further casualties in Norfolk. Zeppelin L14, commanded by Kapitänleutnant der Reserve Alois Böcker, attacked East Dereham on 8 September 1915 and dropped a total of seventy-five bombs, killing five people, injuring many more, and damaging 130 houses, with the heaviest concentration of bombs falling around the Market Place and Church Street. Three of the dead were servicemen from 2/1st City of London Yeomanry.

Damage caused by the Zeppelin raid on the 5th Norfolk's Orderly Headquarters at the corner of Quebec Street in Dereham. (Bishop Bonners Museum)

On 31 January 1916, a total of nine Zeppelins were sent to bomb targets in England and they reached landfall via Norfolk, where bombs were dropped on the coast. The Upcher family of Sheringham House were present for this and recorded that, 'The noise became more distant, seemed [to be] following the coast for a bit, then crash, bang, shake a loud explosion. Every door and window in the house struggling to break free, another and another, then louder.'

Norfolk Constabulary.

PUBLIC NOTICE.

DAYLIGHT
HOSTILE AIR RAIDS

When hostile aircraft are within such a distance of

East Dereham

as to render an attack possible, the public will be warned thereof by the following signals:—

Each Day of the week (including Sunday)
"Danger" Signal.

Three blasts of five seconds each, followed by an interval of one minute, then three more blasts of five seconds each on the "Buzzer" at the Gas Works.

"All Clear" Signal.

One long blast on the "Buzzer."

The signals will be given during the period of **half-an-hour before sunrise to half-an-hour after sunset**. Every effort will be made to give **timely** warning of the approach of hostile aircraft, but the public should remember that the "**Danger**" signal will be given when **Real Danger** is apprehended in which event they should seek shelter with all speed.

Persons still in the open should take what shelter is afforded by lying in ditches, hollows in the ground, &c.

It is recommended that, in the event of raids during school hours, children should be kept in the school until the "**All Clear**" signal is given. Likewise, workpeople at factories, etc., should remain on the premises in whatever shelter is afforded.

Horses and other animals should be stabled or secured in some manner and should not be abandoned in the streets.

J. H. MANDER, Captain,
Chief Constable.

County Police Station,
Castle Meadow, Norwich,
January, 1916.

Air-raid instructions for the population of Dereham. (Norfolk Records Office)

The threats from Zeppelins became an important issue to overcome nationally and Norfolk itself saw a variety of defensive measures put in place. Both the Royal Naval Air Service (RNAS) and the Royal Flying Corps (RFC) made efforts to protect the county from aerial raiders and airfields, such as the one at South Denes in Great Yarmouth, were built up. RNAS 'Satellite' airfields were put into Bacton, Burgh Castle, Narborough and Sedgeford.

The RFC had airfields at Earsham, Freethorpe, Goodnestone Warren, Mousehold Heath, Saxthorpe, Sedgeford, Sporle, Tottenhill, Bircham Newton, Feltwell, Harling Road, Hingham, Marham, Mattishall and West Rudham, and between June and September 1916, 51 Squadron of the Home Defence Wing was based at Snarehill. Pulham would also see a new base for the RNAS, and from here airships carried patrols along the coast and out over the North Sea and the English Channel. From North Walsham, another detachment patrolled the coast around Happisburgh while interceptor stations placed along Norfolk's coastline did sterling work intercepting Zeppelin transmissions and alerting the local populace to impending raids.

An example of what happened during a suspected air raid can be found in the watch minutes for Norwich City Police. On 13 April 1918, an air-raid warning was given and the minutes record, '... at 8.46 p.m. a Field Marshall's order "take air-raid action" was received that 464 Special Constables, 153 Red Cross men, 19 Auxiliary Firemen and 80 Boy Scouts paraded, that the "All Clear" signal was received at 3.26 a.m.' The alert lasted for seven hours.

During these alerts, every effort was made to engage any approaching enemy aircraft. On 27 November 1916, these efforts met with success when pilots, flying from Bacton and Burgh Castle, destroyed Zeppelin L21. The pilots in question were Sub-Lieutenant E.L. Pulling, Flight Lieutenant Egbert Cadbury and Lieutenant W.R. Gayner. All three engaged the Zeppelin, which fell in flames into the sea 10 miles off Lowestoft with no survivors.

Roland le Strange of Hunstanton logged each Zeppelin raid and tried to predict when they would come again. His log shows that in 1915 he predicted eighteen of the twenty-one raids launched on moonlit nights.

Pilots at Snarehill Aerodrome near Thetford. (Norfolk Records Office)

Preparations for Invasion

Defences designed to thwart invasion were constructed along the Norfolk coast and continued inland, often following the course of local rivers. Pillboxes were built throughout the coastal area and many still exist today, although they are often mistaken for their more prolific Second World War counterparts. As the war progressed, emergency measures were planned and posters were put up detailing what action should be taken in the event of an invasion.

Sheringham and Great Yarmouth both lay claim to the first bombs dropping on 19 January 1915, but who is correct? Well, the first bombs fell on Great Yarmouth at around 8.20 p.m. and the first bomb at Sheringham fell at 8.35 p.m. So Great Yarmouth can rightly lay claim to this fact.

The emergency committee of Dersingham, known as Area No. 4, provides a good example of the sort of measures that would come into force if an invasion took place. Public transportation would immediately be rendered useless, removed or taken to its allotted stations. The civilian population would be told to 'Stand-by' and would be expected to pack, while the situation was assessed as either a 'Partial' or

A trooper of the Middlesex Hussars on patrol near Bacton. (Author's collection)

'Total' emergency. Main roads would be closed to civilians so that the military could move freely and civilians would follow a route that took them over the River Ouse at St Germans, Magdalen and Stow. Other routes were provided for the inhabitants of Hunstanton, starting at Rinstead and eventually taking them towards Spalding. There would also be horses readied at Harpley, Appleton, Leziate and East Walton. Finally, it was declared that Special Constables had the same powers as uniformed police and 'must be obeyed'.

At least one invasion alert is mentioned in the diary of the Upcher family, who helped with looking after wounded soldiers at Sheringham Hospital. On 24 February 1916, the Sheringham lifeboat went missing after it had been called out to a ship in distress off Wells. Rumours were rife amongst the soldiers in the hospital and then it was reported that the Germans had landed at Weybourne! 'One further report said that the Germans in khaki having landed were going about shaking hands with soldiers and with the other hand knifing them!'

Reports came in all day and the diary notes that soldiers and their officers were everywhere. One soldier was allowed to put up the Union Jack with the Red Cross flag at the hospital to calm everyone's nerves, but as Upcher states, '… it had the contrary effect on most of them as they again came to pour out their fears that when we are bombarded, "I'm sorry for Sheringham when that happens they will at once fire on the Red Cross flag as they always do."'

The situation was subsequently reported as being 'Normal Conditions', although the lifeboat still had not returned. The craft eventually turned up safe and sound on 27 February; it had encountered some trouble and been forced to go to Grimsby for repairs.

Blackouts

On 12 August 1914, DORA had imposed lighting restrictions under Clause 3 in an effort to deter Zeppelin raids. The initial infractions on lighting in Norfolk were dealt with by cautions but by March 1915 you could be reported and 1,028 offences were recorded for this offence. An example of this can be seen in Inspector Carter's pocket notebook when, on May 1916, he visited a Mrs Gordonshaw of Laburnum House to investigate 'lights seen on 3 occasions'. Further notes reveal that the first occasion involved a light 'shone by a lady living in the house whilst carrying the bath water upstairs' and the following two instances were 'her own light from a window in the front of the house'. Mrs Gordonshaw was reported for these offences.

Stiff penalties were incurred for any infringement and, for the most part, the general public took the blackout very seriously. The possibly of an air strike called for extra vigilance and Fannie Fitt's diary entry for 31 January 1916 notes: 'Zeppelin air raid, all lights turned out at 5–15 p.m. and off until 8 a.m. next morning.'

Enemy raids

Although an invasion never took place, the Germans continued to raid Norfolk and, in total, the county suffered eight hostile night air raids and nineteen Zeppelin fly-overs. It is recorded that 431 high-explosive bombs and 331 incendiary bombs were dropped and five men and two women were killed, with seven men and three women being injured. Damage to properties was estimated at £10,303 7s 6d.

A drawing produced by R.C. Jenkins whilst recovering from wounds. (Norfolk Records Office)

However, the raids did not all come from the air and two more 'seaborne' raids involved Great Yarmouth. The first occurred on 24 April 1916 when 1st Scouting Group – a raiding force of twenty-two capital ships, five older battleships, twelve light cruisers and forty-eight destroyers – sailed towards England under the command of Admiral Boedicker, hoping to draw out their opponents' ships. Unbeknown to the Germans, the British knew this force was on the move. The raid was hampered by Boedicker's flagship, SMS *Seydlitz*, hitting a mine and this delaying the timing of the plan – which was intended to target Lowestoft and Great Yarmouth – for thirty minutes at dawn. The German fleet eventually found itself off Lowestoft at 3.50 a.m. on 25 April, where it tried to entice a British fleet into battle by bombarding the town and causing both heavy damage and a number of casualties. Both fleets now attempted to draw each other away, with the commander of part of the British response – Commodore Tyrwhitt – heading towards Great Yarmouth to thwart any further attacks. The German ships arrived at Great Yarmouth but, as official documents state:

The appearance of our submarines, combined with the Commodore's turn northward, saved Yarmouth from the fate of her sister town. The German light cruisers had turned to the south-east at 4.23, and seven minutes later Commodore Tyrwhitt had sight of them to the north-eastward. He opened fire at 14,000 yards, but all the shots fell short.

Both sides eventually disengaged, with losses to the British of: twenty-five killed, nineteen wounded, two light cruisers damaged, one submarine sunk and 200 houses damaged. Eleven Germans were killed, all from SMS *Seydlitz*, one cruiser was damaged, one submarine sunk and one submarine captured when it beached off Harwich. Great Yarmouth, yet again, had got off lightly.

However, in what became the last German raid seaborne raid on the coast of England, Great Yarmouth did not escape unscathed. At 11.15 p.m. on 14 January 1918, a force of German destroyers appeared off Great Yarmouth and, during a five-minute period, fired over fifty shells into the town, killing four and injuring eight. Official documents note, 'It was only an hour and a half later that Admiral Tyrwhitt put to sea to intercept them, and by then the German destroyers had retired. The intercepting forces saw nothing of the enemy and returned to harbour at noon on the 15th.'

Alfred Sparks (53), his wife Mary (63), John Simpson (17) and Thomas Prigent (42) were all killed and in the inquest that followed, Mary Mildred Pegg, Alfred Sparks' stepdaughter, was called upon to reveal the circumstances of their deaths:

> At about 11 o' clock on the night of the 14th she was sitting in a downstairs room and heard a loud report. Some of the ceiling of the room in which witness was sitting fell upon her. Hearing a cry from upstairs she tried to mount the staircase, but fallen bricks and woodwork stopped her progress.

When Mary was able to get to her parents she found her father sitting up in bed with brickwork and masonry on his legs – he would later die in hospital – and her mother no longer breathing. A statement was also given to relate the events witnessed by Thomas Beesley, master of a local steamer:

> At about five minutes past 11 p.m. on January 14th, when walking with a pilot friend, he heard the German shells and a report from the roadstead. Going on board his ship

he found Simpson dead in his bunk in the forecastle.
Laying about were pieces of shell, broken pieces of iron-
work and splintered wood.

This single shell had entered the deck and exploded outwards.
The inquest came to the conclusion that all four casualties had
died from wounds incurred by the bursting shells discharged
from an enemy warship at sea off the borough.

Conscription

DORA also brought into being the Military Service Act of
1916. The high casualty rate on the Western Front had seen
the rush to join up trickle away and the government decided to
introduce compulsory service for all single men aged between
16 and 41. The act did, however, allow men to appeal against
military service on religious, political or moral grounds. Many
of these who appealed went on to serve in non-combatant roles,
becoming stretcher-bearers or working in munitions factories.
But others refused to be involved in the war in any way and
these became known as 'Absolutists'. As casualties mounted,
the act was amended in May 1916 to include married men and,
by April 1918, the upper age limit rose to include men as old
as 56. This prompted many older men to appeal against being
drafted into the army.

The authorities were prepared to listen to those who wanted
to state their case and they could do so either by sitting at a
Military Service Tribunal or having their case heard at a Court
Martial. Both were heard all over Norfolk. One man who went
through this process was Robert Artis of Gorleston, who was
a fish smoker and curer by trade. Robert's case was heard at
3.30 p.m. on Wednesday, 8 March 1916 at Great Yarmouth
Town Hall.

It is apparent that his hearing decided that he could be
considered for military service because he was exempted from
'Combatant Service Only'. Robert appealed this decision but

The tribunals held to hear men's cases against being conscripted evolved as the war went on. Initially, the ones held in Norwich gave the men a number, perhaps to provide anonymity. However, by mid-May of 1916, this had changed and each man was named.

the tribunal refused any further discussion and he enlisted with the Non-Combatant Corps (NCC) on 27 May 1916. He served the entire war as a groundsman with No. 1 Company NCC at Aldershot until he was discharged on 16 December 1919.

A tribunal held in King's Lynn looked at the local grocers in Dereham and their continued exemption from military service. Presided over by Lord Kimberly and Lieutenant L.W.J. Costello, the enquiry focused on four grocers aged between 33 and 40. Once their cases had been reviewed, one man was allowed to continue his exemption but the other three were ordered to report for military service. One of the men was 33 years old and married with two children; he was declared medically fit and Lieutenant Costello stated:

There are still eighteen grocers in Dereham of military age, and others above military age. They have granted this man exemption until December 27th, 1917. How is this war to be finished if local tribunals deal with A1 men in this way? The military appeal was allowed and the man was ordered to serve on September 18th.

Another example involves two men from the Great Eastern Railway (GER). James Wright, a shunter at Dereham, was instructed to attend a medical board on 22 January 1917, having been on the army reserve list since November 1915. He was enlisted into the Royal Engineers and found himself serving with the 99th Light Railway Company. But Mr W.F. Wright, a railway manager of the GER at Norwich, carried a card that exempted him. The card stated that, '… your services are required in connection with the Railway' and if he was called up he had been told to, '… shew him this card, give him any particulars he may require, and ask him to communicate with the Railway Company if he has any doubts'. Mr Wright was not called to enlist.

GREAT EASTERN RAILWAY.

14901

2 JUL 1918

To _W. F. Wright_

Department _Chief Traffic Manager's_

Station _Norwich_

You are hereby informed that your services are required in connection with the Railway. You will not, therefore, at present be required to join the Army, but should you receive a notice calling you up, you should report to the Recruiting Officer who has sent you the notice and shew him this Card, give him any particulars he may require, and ask him to communicate with the Railway Company if he has any doubts. This Card has been issued with the approval of the War Office.

Exd. _WRf_

H. W. Thornton
General Manager.

Exemption card for Great Eastern Railway staff (William Marriott Museum)

Some local residents had different views about how the war should be handled and perhaps one of the most vocal was James Frederick 'Fred' Henderson, who was a British socialist writer and Labour Party politician from Norwich. His political writings were included in the _Herald_ dated 27 March 1915: 'Either we are out to win a new life through all this, we Europeans, or we are loathsome, the very scum of murder and degeneracy.' Henderson believed that everyone was in the war together and that 'National Unity' had to stand as the 'New Faith'. By the middle of 1918 this had effectively become fact.

Temperance

DORA was also used to control the consumption of alcohol and by October 1915 the government had brought in a number of measures including a 'No Treating Order', which stated that you could not buy alcoholic drinks for other people. Opening times were also reduced to 12.00–2.30 p.m. and 6.30–9.30 p.m., with beer being watered down and an extra penny in tax put on a pint of beer. These were not popular measures and Fred Henderson noted that many believed it was:

> To divert attention from this fundamental thing by abusing sections of our working population for drinking, is the most fatal folly. It has already produced a widespread resentment, which may seriously worsen the position; resentment which is greater because the average workman suspects that the thing is being done by deliberate intention to divert criticism away from private profiteering.

In this way, DORA were aiding the Temperance League who were against drunkenness and excess, and who called for total abstinence from alcohol. George Edwards, the Primitive Methodist Norfolk agriculturist, talked about temperance in a sermon read at Sculthorpe on 14 November 1915. In it he cited that strong alcohol would bring three main things: disgrace, disease and death. He concluded, 'My last point is [that] strong drink brings death, it has been stated on very high authority that we have 60,000 deaths in the United Kingdom in one year caused by drink [and] that is very near as many deaths we have had through this war.'

Rationing

As the war progressed, another sacrifice that had to be made on the home front was rationing. The Ministry of Food introduced restrictions on foodstuffs in January 1918 when the U-boat war impacted upon the importation of such products. Sugar and meat were both rationed and permits decreed that '... in one amount you were not to exceed 2 oz per head per day for a period of 4 days'. The regulations also applied to those who served in the military and everybody had to register with a butcher. The butcher D.W. Bellamy, at No. 136 King Street in Great Yarmouth, issued small cards to each customer who registered with them. These cards were a declaration that each adult or child was not registered with another butcher. Registrations had to be lodged by 13 March and the rules of selling meat were very specific, with instructions issued to D.W. Bellamy under the Meat Rationing Order 1918 stating, 'On and after April 7th, no general butcher may sell beef, mutton or pork (including suet and all edible offal), except to an individual who has registered his card with the butcher …'

Local Food Control Committees were set up and they had the power to limit the number of customers accepted by butchers. These local committees had to form themselves into a Butchers' Committee and appoint one buyer of livestock and one buyer of dead meat to act on behalf of all the members of the committee. In essence this meant that no one without a permit could buy meat wholesale. By August 1918, petrol was being rationed for vehicles carrying goods and this also had a bearing on butchers.

A child's ration book from 1918. (Gressinghall Museum)

MINISTRY OF FOOD.
CHILD'S RATION BOOK (A).

INSTRUCTIONS.

Read carefully these instructions and the leaflet which will be sent you with this Book.

1. The parent or guardian of the child named on the reference leaf as the holder of this ration book must sign his own name and write the child's name and address in the space below, and write the child's name and address, and the serial number (printed upside down on the back cover) in the space provided to the left of each page of coupons.

Food Office of } Issue .... **AYLSHAM.** Date 2 NOV 1918

Signature of Child's } Parent or Guardian **Ellen Payne**

Name of Child **Kathleen M. Payne**

Address **Heydon**

2. For convenience of writing at the Food Office the Reference Leaf has been put opposite the back cover, and has purposely been printed upside down. It should be carefully examined. If there is any mistake in the entries on the Reference Leaf, the Food Office should be asked to correct it.

3. The book must be registered at once by the child's parent or guardian, who must take the book to the retailers with whom the child was previously registered for butcher's meat, bacon, butter and margarine, sugar and tea respectively, or, if the child has not previously held a book, to any retailers chosen. These retailers must write their names and the addresses of their shops in the proper space on the back of the cover. The books of children staying in hotels, boarding houses, hostels, schools and similar establishments should not be registered until they leave the establishment.

4. The ration book may be used only by or on behalf of the holder, to buy rationed food for him, or members of the same household, or guests sharing common meals. It may not be used to buy rationed food for any other persons.

N. 1 (Nov.) [*Continued on next page.*

IF FOUND, RETURN TO ANY FOOD OFFICE.

Wilson Stockings, who had a butcher's at St Stephens, had to carry a permit in order to deliver meat with the Road Transport Order 1918 which allowed them to trade by the use of a van. These limitations were accepted by the public as a necessary part of the war effort.

Coping with the Conflict

Families learned to cope with the news of their loved ones going missing or being killed in many ways. The Hewetson family experienced this when Phillip went missing in June 1918. Ruth believed he had been captured by the enemy and wrote to her parents in an effort to comfort them: 'I think it just too splendid to think of that little band led by him fighting all on their own for all that time and oh I do think it really does sound as if he were a prisoner.' William Hewetson, meanwhile, sought solace and support from God and his parish work. He noted in the parish magazine for Wroxham in July 1918:

> The shadow of a great Cross encircles us. 'I, if I be lifted up will draw all men unto me' and so it is we are united. The nation is being drawn together through the power of the Cross.' 'For we know that the whole creation groaneth and travaileth together in pain until now.' Will the pain and sorrow purify?

Many others looked to entertainment for a distraction from the pain that wartime brought and attended shows at the Hippodrome in Norwich. Fannie Fitt, who was married to the owner, William, kept a diary throughout the war. Every week the theatre provided some form of amusement or diverting attraction with, for instance, a '"Shell-Out" at Hippo. Good first House & decent second at Hip.' on Monday, 27 November 1916 and, on Monday, 8 July 1918, 'Revue Buds & Blossoms at Hippo'. Later that week, Fannie jotted down that, 'Business [was] very good'.

A number of other institutions also provided entertainment and Fannie helped out at both the YMCA and the VAD, noting in her diary on 27 April 1916 that they 'Took all the artistes to the War Hospital (Norfolk) to give wounded our special matinee.'

Soldiers were also keen to fill their time of leave with activity. James Neville was able to take time away from the front line whilst recovering from jaundice and gastritis and he writes that, 'Yesterday Dick and I went and two others went up the river in a small rowing boat and had tea in a small pub. In the evening we had a very expensive dinner in town.' Aware that the time to return would soon come, James writes: 'It's good-bye to civilisation but I feel that my luck is still in.'

THE BLACKOUT

Of all the precautions taken by Norfolk in the First World War, it seems quite clear that the lighting restrictions under Clause 3 of DORA were a key part of thwarting hostile raids on Norwich. A mixture of severe penalties and the fact that the general public took the blackout quite seriously meant that the restrictions were maintained conscientiously.

Frederick Eaton notes the success of the blackout during the war:

> ... there were many raids and warnings of raids. Not once was a bomb dropped upon the city. I have stood in the streets on more than one occasion when the Zeppelins buzzed over the city. I feel confident that even if the specials did make themselves a nuisance to usually law abiding citizens they saved the city from damage by hostile bombs.

As Eaton says, although the air-raid warning was sounded for Norwich – most notably on 31 January and 1 October 1916 – not one bomb fell on the city. The raid in January saw nine Zeppelins being ordered to attack targets all over England, but the only bombs recorded falling on Norfolk were around Sheringham.

The closest the city came to an attack was the raid in October when Zeppelins were seen over Cotessey and Magdalen Police Station. On this night, eleven Zeppelins had been sent to raid England and bombs were dropped 5 miles out at Easton Park. Norfolk Constabulary records support the belief that the effective blackout throughout the city, along with detailed air-raid preparations, contributed to the failure of these Zeppelins to locate Norwich. 'Unquestionably this represented the narrowest escape Norwich had from being bombed, and the greatest credit was due to the police authorities for the alertness and resources which they displayed in meeting the emergency.'

COUNTY OF NORFOLK.

DEFENCE OF THE REALM

Local Emergency Committee.

Local Emergency Committees have been formed in the County of Norfolk, acting under a Central Emergency Committee, of which the Lord Lieutenant is Chairman, whose duty is to act with the Military Authorities in case of invasion, which, though improbable, cannot be ignored, and renders it necessary that arrangements should be made for the conduct of the Civil Population. The details of the local arrangements are left to the Local Emergency Committees to carry out through the Police and Special Constables.

The following instructions are issued by the Emergency Committee of the _____ Pulham _____ Police Division, and have been approved by the Central Committee and authorised by the Military Authorities:—

1. REMOVAL OF TRANSPORT.

It is most imperative that no horses of useable age, waggons, carts, traction engines, motors, petrol, harness, etc., should be allowed to fall into the hands of the enemy for transport purposes. As far as possible they should all be removed on the general lines of evacuation as stated in paragraph 3, taking the aged and infirm, etc., with them.

All carts, etc., which cannot be removed must be rendered useless by sawing a piece out of half the spokes in each wheel. (These instructions do not apply to horses, carts, or other transport which has been commandeered by the Military Authorities, and the orders of the latter in respect thereof must be strictly carried out.)

2. EVACUATION OF THE CIVIL POPULATION.

Except in places where evacuation is suggested by the Military Authorities, all members of the Civil Population must decide for themselves whether they prefer to remain at home, or to retreat inland. If they remain at home they must on no account use firearms.

In case of a raid, word will be passed round to "Stand by," when all persons intending to leave their homes should pack their carts, etc., with warm clothes, blankets, and enough provisions for about two days.

The above message may be followed by "Partial Emergency," "Total Emergency," or "As you were."

If "Partial Emergency" is sent, all vehicles previously earmarked for any duties will at once be sent to their allotted stations; all serviceable horses, vehicles, petrol, etc., in the area will be moved inland or rendered unserviceable.

If "Total Emergency" is sent out, all the measures arranged for by the Emergency Committees are to be put at once into complete execution.

3. LINES OF EVACUATION.

Most of the MAIN roads will be closed to civilians, being reserved for the use of the Military. Should troops wish to come along a road, all civil traffic must at once draw to one side or get into adjoining fields, leaving the road clear.

All traffic from the above-named district must proceed towards _____ Thetford. _____

The roads available for the retreat of the inhabitants of _____ Fersfield _____

will be via _____ South-west to South Lopham; or North to Fersfield Common, _____ and North-west to Kenninghall.

4. MOVEMENT OF USEABLE HORSES.

Concentration camps for horses will be at _____ Quidenham _____

5. SPECIAL CONSTABLES HAVE THE FULL POWERS OF UNIFORMED POLICE AND MUST BE OBEYED.

They will do their best to tell _____ which roads to move by, and the situation of rest and feeding stations.

6. The name of the Emergency Special Constable responsible for the parish of _____ Fersfield _____ is _____ R. F. Bennett, _____ The Row, _____ from whom further information can be obtained.

BY ORDER OF THE LORD LIEUTENANT AND THE EXECUTIVE COMMITTEE OF THE CENTRAL EMERGENCY COMMITTEE.

NORWICH,
April 2nd, 1917.

J. H. MANDER, Captain,
Chief Constable.

GOD SAVE THE KING.

FLETCHER & SON, LTD., PRINTERS, NORWICH.

This DORA poster tells residents around Pulham what they should do in the event of an invasion. (Norfolk Constabulary Historical Collection)

6

COMING HOME

By April 1918, the war on the Western Front had moved to Flanders, where the 9/Norfolks took part in the Battle of the Lys. Here they defended Crucifix Corner, situated to the east of Ballieul, and aided the 4/Lincolnshires in repulsing a number of determined German counter-attacks.

A few months later, in August 1918, the tide turned in favour of the Allied forces with the launch of their own offensive at Amiens beginning on 8 August. On this day the 7/Norfolks took part in the subsidiary attack facing Morlancourt, where all objectives were met. Archie Milk went over the top this day with his battalion at Hourges. The 52nd Battalion's war diary stated:

> The attacking battalions of the Brigade moving forward very rapidly and numerous small bodies of the enemy, passed in the fog, were encountered by the various companies of the Battalion. These were dealt with in detail, prisoners and machine guns being taken ... During the attack the Battalion's casualties were, unfortunately, fairly heavy, Lieutenants A.P. Milk, M.M. and J. Langford, killed ...

Archie is now laid to rest in grave A.68 in Hourges Orchard Cemetery, close to where he fell.

By now the Germans were beginning to retreat. On 18 August, the 12/Norfolks – who had been formed from the 1/1st Norfolk Yeomanry and now served with the 94th Brigade in the 31st Division – took part in the Battle of Outersteene Ridge, gaining all of their objectives and reaching the Outersteene-Vieux-Berquin road. At the old Somme battlefield, the 7/Norfolks formed part of the advancing Allied force and, on 25 August, they assisted in the capture of a line of trenches around Carnoy. On 28 August their headquarters were shelled during their relief of the 1/Cambridgeshires and 'several of the runners and signallers were killed or wounded'.

Edgar Gray was a signaller for the battalion. By 3 September he was in Blighty and it is said that he won a Military Medal for carrying wounded officers back to their lines, but got drunk that night and was nearly court martialled for laying a wreath on someone's bed. He was rightly awarded the Military Medal on 11 February 1919. Known as 'Jack the Lad', he died in an accident in 1948.

Edgar Gray served in the 7/ Norfolks and won the Military Medal. (Courtesy of Steve Crisp)

END OF THE WAR.

ARMISTICE SIGNED AT 5 A.M.

HOSTILITIES CEASED AT 11 A.M.

The Prime Minister makes the following announcement:—

The armistice was signed at 5 a.m. this morning, and hostilities are to cease on all fronts at 11 am.

The Armistice as reported in the EDP on 11 November 1918. (EDP)

By September the Germans were in continual retreat and the 1/Norfolks found themselves assisting in the capture of Delsaux Farm near Beugny. The 7/Norfolks were at Nurlu on 5 September and both the 7th and 9th Battalions took part in some heavy fighting during the Battle of Epehy on 18 September, which saw that position eventually fall to the 35th Brigade. Like many of the men in the British Expeditionary Force, the Norfolks battalions could not believe the news when they finally heard that the Armistice had been signed on 11 November 1918. The war diary for the 7/Norfolks, who were at Landas, simply recorded the cease fire as, 'At 8 a.m. news comes through that the Armistice has been signed coming into operation at 11 o'clock this morning.'

Such a short statement upon this momentous occasion suggests that the writer, along with those at home, may still have been taking stock of the last four years of war. All regiments were soon rejoicing at the thought of returning home to their loved ones, although the filtering of troops back to Britain would be gradual and far slower than some would have liked. As peace finally reigned, the 1/Norfolks were at Le Quesnoy and the 9/Norfolks were positioned at Bohain, where soon afterwards they became part of the British forces that would march to the Rhine.

At home, the news that the war was over was commented on by Fannie Fitt: 'Up in good time for the joyful news that the armistice had been signed about 10.20 a.m. Great excitement everywhere and very full houses at night at the Hippo.'

George Hardingham, who had served at the front since April 1915, wrote in a letter dated 19 November 1918:

Well the war is finished and I'm looking forward to having a good time in the future. I'm thankful to have got right through without any serious injury ... The news is really too good to realise, one can't imagine the war is over and I'm sure I shan't until I'm in civilian clothes again.

Sam Gall, serving with the Machine Gun Corps, wrote to his sweetheart Louisa 'Louie' Smith on 12 November 1918:

My dearest Louie, Hoping this card will find you all in the pink … I arrived in Ripon yesterday that was Monday but I don't think I am stopping here above 2 or 3 days. Will send my address as soon as I can and I know that you were pleased to hear it is all over.

They had sent postcards to each other all through 1918 – conducting their romance by letter and postcard since they could rarely meet – and were married in 1923.

Many families lost at least one close relative during the war. Corporal George Hardingham, writing to his family on 22 June 1916, informed them: 'Well, we are expecting to be making a move now shortly, so I am writing to tell you all to be of good cheer, and to put your trust in God, for He is the only Giver of Victory, and He can save by many, or by few.' He ended the letter by saying, 'Good-bye, and God bless you all'. Nine days after this letter was written George was dead, killed in the first few hours of the Battle of the Somme. He has no known grave and is commemorated on the Thiepval Memorial. George's mother and father inscribed these words on a memorial card: 'Killed in action, our hearts are sore, As time goes on we miss him more, His tender smile, his loving face, No one on earth can fill his place.'

Others were luckier. Albert Statham won the Distinguished Conduct Medal (DCM) along with the Military Medal and Bar while serving with the 34 Divisional Signals. His DCM was won on 14/15 October 1918 for keeping phone lines open at Gheluvelt during the capture of Menin. Part of his citation reads, 'He was severely wounded on the 15th October in the performance of these duties. He did

A postcard sent by Sam Gall to Louisa Smith on 12 November 1918. (Courtesy of Mike and Muriel Fuller)

I long to be with you, dear Heart, But countless miles us sever, So send this token just to prove A love that lasts for ever.

FROM MY HEART

fine work.' He was able to return to the GPO after the war but never spoke about his experiences during the war to his son.

The spy-hunting Chief Constable of Norfolk County, Egbert Napier, did not survive the war. He had got his wish and rejoined the army, landing in France on 14 October 1916 where, one month later, he was killed in action on 13 November while leading elements of the 5/Gordon Highlanders at Beaumont Hamel on the Somme. His passing was reported in the news and he was commemorated as '… a soldierly figure at all times'.

The Cobb family saw both tragedy and survival. Harry was wounded at Fromelles on 19 July 1916 serving with the 2/6 Gloucestershire Regiment and died of his wounds on 30 July. Willie was discharged from the Australian Army on 13 April 1920 and had by then returned to Woodford in Australia. Charlie was discharged on 19 March 1919 and joined Willie in Australia, where he became involved with the Australian Returned Soldiers League and by 1926 he was vice president of the Woodford

Crowds gathering in North Walsham on 11 November 1918 after the Armistice had been signed. (Gressinghall Museum)

Branch. Sadly, Gladys (aged 23) died of influenza and toxic jaundice at Stoner Camp on 12 February 1919, in an epidemic that killed more people than the war itself.

And what of the 5/Norfolks who had disappeared? Local papers recorded their loss as early on as 27 August 1915 when the *Lynn Advertiser* reported, 'It is with the deepest regret that we publish the list of missing officers of the 5th (Territorial) Battalion of the Norfolk Regiment. At the time of going to press, no further information is available than the bare fact that they are missing.'

Albert Statham served in the 34th Divisional Signals and won the Distinguished Conduct Medal and the Military Medal and Bar. (Courtesy of Gerald Statham)

William Cobb served with the 23rd Company Australian Army Service Corps. (Courtesy of Nick Cobb)

A little while later, casualty lists appeared and, in the succeeding weeks, these recorded the names of the officers and men who were wounded, killed or missing, including the names of thirteen others who were reported as being prisoners of war. However, on 6 January 1916, a dispatch written by Sir Ian Hamilton was published questioning what had happened to the Norfolks. He ended by stating, '… Nothing more was ever seen or heard of any of them. They charged into the forest and were lost to sight or sound. Not one of them ever came back.'

Even the king, who sent a cable to Hamilton at some point towards the end of September 1915, became involved: 'I am most anxious to be informed as to the fate of men of the 5th Battalion Norfolk Regiment as they include my agent Captain Frank Beck and the Sandringham Company.'

Today, it is believed that Beck, and a number of the men who advanced, were summarily executed by the Turks. Although it was assumed that these men all came from Sandringham, in reality this battalion was recruited from all over North Norfolk. At the time the *Lynn News* disputing Hamilton's report:

At Norwich the authorities whose business it is to complete the statistical abstracts could not at the outset make the figure any higher than 177. Of these 137 are still unaccounted for. There thus remains a balance of 40 men, of whom the following two officers and thirteen men now known to be prisoners of war in Turkey while the remaining 25 are dead or in the hospitals of the Allies, or are known to be otherwise safe …

Harry Cobb died of wounds on 19 July 1916 while serving with the 2/6 Gloucestershire Regiment. (Courtesy of Nick Cobb)

Witnesses who were actually there, such as Private Sidney Pooley, totally refuted the disappearance: 'I did not see any wood into which the officers and men could have disappeared, and I certainly did not see them charge into a wood; in fact the Norfolks did not charge as far as my knowledge goes. I know absolutely nothing about how the officers and men disappeared.'

In fact, they lay where they fell until 1919 when the battalion's chaplain, the Reverend Pierrepoint Edwards, found them:

We have found the 5th Norfolks – there were 180 in all; 122 Norfolk and a few Hants and Suffolks with 2/4th Cheshires. We could only identify two – Privates Barnaby and Carter. They were scattered over an area of about one square mile, at a distance of at least 800 yards behind the Turkish front line. Many of them had evidently been killed in a farm, as a local Turk, who owns the place, told us that when he came back he found the farm covered with the decomposing bodies of British soldiers, which he threw into a small ravine. The whole thing quite bears out the original theory that they did not go very far on, but got mopped up one by one, all except the ones who got into the farm.

Buried in a mass grave in Azmak Cemetery, Suvla, the names of these men were commemorated on the Helles memorial.

Ironically, Peter Strasser – commander of the Zeppelin raid of 19 January 1915 – would perish off Wells-next-the-Sea in Zeppelin L70 during the last raid of the war. Egbert Cadbury would be the pilot and, along with his gunner Captain Robert Leckie and Lieutenant Edward Keys, rightly earned a Distinguished Flying Cross for bringing down the Zeppelin. Their citation states:

> These officers attacked and destroyed a large enemy airship which recently attempted a raid on the North-East Coast, and also succeeded in damaging a second airship. The services rendered on this occasion were of the greatest value, and the personal risk was very considerable for aeroplanes a long way out from land.

Peter Strasser perished in Zeppelin L70 when it was shot down off Wells on 5 August 1918. (Author's collection)

Egbert Cadbury and Robert Leckie, pictured soon after they had landed after bringing down Zeppelin L70. (Author's collection)

EDGAR
SPEYER

Previously accused of spying for the enemy, Edgar Speyer was tried under the British Nationality and Status of Aliens Act 1918 and found guilty of 'disloyalty and disaffection' and condemned for reputedly having 'unlawfully communicated with subjects of an enemy State and associated with business and that he, "has shown himself by act and speech to be disaffected and disloyal to His Majesty"'. Speyer and his family lost their British nationality and he was struck off the roll of the Privy Council. Speyer maintained his innocence throughout and, in *The Times* on 9 January 1922, he stated, '... the whole thing is neither more nor less than the culmination of years of political persecution. The Home Secretary simply dared not give me the vindication to which I was entitled.'

Sir Edgar Speyer and Lady Leonora Speyer pictured around 1921.
(Illustrated London News)

Victoria Cross

Six men connected with Norfolk won the Victoria Cross (VC). They were Harry M. Daniels (Wymondham), Harry Cator (Drayton), Sidney James Day (Norwich), John Sherwood-Kelly (Norfolk Regiment), Arthur Henry Cross (Shipdham) and Gordon Muriel Flowerdew (Scole).

Company Sergeant Major 9665 Harry M. Daniels joined the Rifle Brigade at 18 and by 12 March 1915 was serving in France. On this day, during the Battle of Neuve Chappelle, Harry was awarded the VC with his friend Cecil Noble for cutting wire under heavy fire. 'A few minutes later Noble was hit in the chest; Daniels moved him to a shell hole and applied first aid, staying with him until help arrived. Noble died of wounds the next day.'

Harry Daniel on a visit to Norwich after he was awarded the Victoria Cross in 1916. (Author's collection)

Harry became a local hero and was presented with a purse of gold by the sheriff. He received a commission and was awarded the Military Cross in 1916. He remained in the army after the war and died in Leeds on 13 December 1953.

Lieutenant Colonel John Sherwood-Kelly was born in Queenstown in South Africa on 13 January 1880. At the age of 37 he was an acting lieutenant colonel in the Norfolk Regiment but in command of the 1st Battalion Royal Inniskilling Fusiliers. On 20 November 1917, during the Battle of Cambrai, he led his men with great bravery. Part of his citation reads, 'He took a Lewis gun team, forced his way through obstacles and covered the advance of his battalion, enabling them to capture the position.'

During the war a total of 30,457 men passed through Thorpe Station in Norfolk, which had a purpose-built restroom dedicated to the wounded.

John would serve in Northern Russia in 1919, where he was court martialled on 28 October for contravening the King's Regulations for writing letters to the press opposing Britain's involvement in the campaign. An article printed in the *Melbourne Argus* on 15 February 1941 noted:

> The sentence of the court martial added the journalist was a severe reprimand but it meant the end of Sherwood-Kelly's military career. I never heard what became of him, but those who knew him and understood the motives behind his extraordinary action in relinquishing his command in North Russia will always honour him as a very gallant and high minded soldier.

John Sherwood-Kelly died on 18 August 1931 and was given a full military funeral at Brookwood Military Cemetery.

Sergeant 5190 Harry Cator served with the 7th Battalion East Surrey Regiment. He won his VC on 9 April 1917, during the Arras Offensive, for capturing a machine gun and then holding the position with a Lewis gun. 'He continued to hold that end of the trench with the Lewis gun and with such effect that the bombing squad was enabled to work along, the result being that one hundred prisoners and five machine guns were captured.' Harry survived the war and died on 7 April 1966.

Corporal Sidney James Day served with the 11th Battalion Suffolk Regiment and won his VC east of Hargicourt on 26 August 1917. Part of his citation reads: 'The corporal seized the bomb and threw it over the trench where it immediately exploded. He afterwards completed the clearing of the trench and established himself in an advanced position, remaining for 66 hours at his post which came under intense fire.'

After the war, Sidney became a butcher before opening a tearoom in Landport called 'Sidney James VC Tea Rooms'. However, this was destroyed in the Second World War and he worked in Portsmouth Dockyard until he had to retire through ill health in 1948. Sidney died in Queen Alexandra's Hospital on 17 July 1959 and is buried in Milton Cemetery with his wife Doris.

Corporal 62990 Arthur Henry Cross served with the 40th Battalion Machine Gun Corps and won his VC on 25 March 1918 at Ervillers for capturing prisoners and causing heavy casualties in a counter-attack. Part of his citation reads: 'It is impossible to speak too highly of the extreme gallantry and dash displayed by this NCO who showed throughout four days of operations, supreme devotion to duty.'

After the war, Arthur devoted a lot of his time to the Machine Gun Corps Old Comrades' Association. He died in 1965.

Lieutenant Gordon Muriel Flowerdew was born on 2 January 1885 and moved to Canada in 1903. He received a commission with Lord Strathcona's Horse (Royal Canadians) and on 30 March 1918 he was leading C Squadron near Moreuil Wood when two lines of German infantry were seen. He ordered the squadron to charge them; passing through their ranks twice and effectively breaking this enemy force. However, their success came at a cost, with the squadron suffering 70 per cent casualties. Lieutenant Flowerdew was 'dangerously wounded through both thighs during the operation, but continued to cheer on his men. There can be no doubt that this officer's great valour was the prime factor in the capture of the position.'

Sadly, Gordon died of the wounds he received during this action the following day. He was 32 and is now laid to rest in grave I.H.1. at Namps-au-Val Cemetery.

Shell Shock

Those that survived often had to contend with the symptoms of what became known as 'shell shock', suffering terrible mental breakdowns as a result of their experiences. Shell shock often took time to manifest itself and men often experienced months of the horrors of trench warfare before they succumbed. James Neville wrote, 'I'm not much looking forward to being under fire again and though I've had a good rest, it makes one more windy because one has forgotten what it is like.' One sufferer described his reaction to a dawn counter-attack less than forty-eight hours after he had seen 70 per cent of his battalion decimated: 'I lost control when I went into the dugout and concealed myself, and also for that week in which I could not control my tears …'

But the authorities were reluctant to admit to the mental effects of warfare. Men suffering from shell shock were shot for cowardice or court martialled even though the term was mentioned in an article in *The Lancet* as early as February 1915. It was not until 1922 that a final report was published after a War Office Committee had looked into the matter. The report summed up its findings as follows: 'No human being, however constituted, however free from inherent weakness, however highly trained to meet the stress and strain and the wear and tear of modern warfare can resist the direct effect of the bursting of high explosive shells.'

This did not stop the committee from concluding that proper training and recruitment would help to minimise future cases of what was also termed 'war-neurosis'. Nevertheless, the recognition of shell shock would ultimately lead to 114,600 men applying for war pensions under its heading.

Five men died of their wounds or died of illness on 11 November 1918 who can be traced back to Norfolk. These are Frederick Charles Bayles from Diss, Walter George Earl from Gimingham, Charles William Frost from King's Lynn, Maurice Leavold from Blickling and Thomas Mayes from Thorpe Market.

Phillip Hewetson

Sadly, Phillip Hewetson never made it home to his beloved family. His father, William Hewetson, was told:

> His unit put up a splendid fight, which lasted about three quarters of an hour. By that time they were almost surrounded. One officer and a few men managed to fight their way through. Your son was last seen alive by this officer, and there is every possibility he was taken prisoner.

When he was reported missing in June 1918, his sister Ruth maintained hope: 'I've got a really strong feeling that our dear Phillip is a prisoner and I don't believe we shall never meet again as a whole family somehow that feeling is there and I don't lose it.'

This reunion, however, was not to be. Phillip had been wounded during the terrible fighting around the Chemin des Dames, which took place between 28 May and 2 June 1918. The 9/Loyal North Lancashires incurred heavy casualties after the Germans had managed to cross the River Aisne at Maizy and it was during this struggle that Phillip was captured. He died of septicaemia and dysentery in a German hospital at Beaurieux on 3 July 1918. He is now laid to rest in Vendresse British Cemetery in France.

A Return to Normality?

It would take Britain many years to return to some semblance of normality following the war. Companies were no longer required to manufacture wartime articles and returned to many of their previous industries; buildings that had been damaged or had temporarily served as hospitals and training grounds were restored; and lives were slowly pieced back together, although many of the scars produced by the conflict would never truly heal.

Rationing continued, even though the war had ended, and Tom Eaton was sent to investigate a crowd of people who were gathered outside a grocer's shop in Norwich. He later wrote: 'I observed a crowd of some one hundred men and women outside a greengrocer's shop. After enquiries I heard that the people were waiting for dates!' The crowds were eventually satisfied and Eaton noted that the dates were being sold for 6*d* a pound and that around 300 people managed to get one bag each!

With men returning from the front it was no longer necessary for women to continue filling traditional male roles in the workplace. Nevertheless, the war had changed the lives of women on the home front in two main ways: firstly by allowing them into occupations which had previously been barred to them, and secondly by establishing separate women's unions with female trade union membership increasing from 357,000 in 1914 to over 1 million by 1918. Another milestone was reached in 1918, with the Representation of the People Act enabling 8.4 million women to have the vote. William Hewetson wrote:

> A certain number of women are for the future to have a voice in the making of her laws. The men are dying for her. Will women rise up and make her worthy of her sacrifice? Then they must read, mark, learn and pray for wisdom to use their vote aright. And then they must use it.

Although this Act only gave the vote to a limited number of women, the Great War had allowed many women to find independence. Ruth Hewetson, for instance, became a scripture mistress at Bedford High School and was involved in the Girl Guides Association until her death in 1983.

Two families lost four sons each. These were Arthur, Clifford, Horace and Royden Bird from East Runton and Charles, George, Horace and Thomas Creasey from West Runton. Charles and Thomas Creasey and Arthur, Clifford and Horace Bird were lost serving with the 5/Norfolks at the 2nd Battle of Gaza.

THE SIEGE OF KUT-AL-AMARA

Of all the tragedies that would be learnt after the cessation of hostilities, it is the experiences of the 2/Norfolks at Kut that comes to mind immediately. After the failed attack on Ctesiphon in November 1915, Sir Charles Townshend, the commander of the 6th (Poona) Division, led his beleaguered force to Kut-al-Amara to form a line of defence. They occupied the town on 3 December 1915 and by 7 December, Turkish forces arrived and laid siege.

The 2/Norfolks headquarters occupied a building called the Serai and they dug in to await relief. The daily routine would see the men manning trenches, coming under fire from artillery and working on fatigue parties. Townshend estimated he had supplies for a month; however, this eventually had to be stretched to five months.

Christmas Eve saw the Turks attack and occupy parts of the town, January 1916 saw floods and terrible conditions and in February the daily rations per man were reduced to three-quarters while the Turks continued to heavily shell the town and attack from the air.

By March it was learnt that all relief efforts were suspended and scurvy broke out. Horses were being used for food and many supplies had run out. By April, malnutrition had begun to set in and on 26 April – 146 days after the siege had started – Townshend surrendered the garrison. The Norfolks went into captivity, where many were treated terribly. It was a testament to the battalion that General Hamilton noted of them, 'In spite of all the trying conditions of the prolonged siege, the discipline, good order, and soldierly bearing of the battalion were maintained to the end.'

During the siege the 2/Norfolks lost seventy-three men and it is estimated that 310 men went into captivity.

The 2|Norfolks after their return from Mesopotamia. This picture was taken on 11 April 1919 during their 'Welcome Home' parade. (Norfolk Constabulary Historical Collection)

Postscript

Legacy

In 1934, a book called *Covenants with Death* was published in an effort to show the true horrors of the Great War. It listed Britain's losses as 2,397,994 killed or wounded on the Western Front and 311,968 killed or wounded serving in other theatres, as well as the losses incurred by the Royal Navy. Added together, this produced a total of 2,709,962 casualties for the Great War, with other sources suggesting that the figure could be as much as 3,190,235. In total, 14,889 Norfolk men were either killed, wounded or invalided as a result of the conflict. Globally, it is estimated that 59,529,331 people were killed, wounded or reported missing. It is little wonder then, that the generation that experienced the war felt the need to remember their fallen.

One early representation of public grief came when a memorial to Edith Cavell was unveiled on 12 October 1918 by Queen Alexandra in Tombland. A similar reaction was recorded when Edith's body was escorted back to England on HMS *Rowena*, landing at Dover on 14 May 1919 prior to being taken to Westminster Abbey for a service of remembrance the following day. Her execution by the Germans was still a very raw subject and Rider Haggard noted in his war diary on 14 October 1918: 'It is now reported, on what seems excellent authority, that the evidence against Edith Cavell was extracted from a sister nurse of sonnambulic tendencies by mesmerism.'

This, of course, is not true, but it is not surprising that such misinformation was reported at a time when her execution was being globally criticised. When her body was finally escorted to London, there was a public outpouring of grief throughout Britain, with *The Times* recording:

> At almost every station along the way and at windows near the railway and by the bridges there were crowds of children quietly and reverently watching the passing. Schoolboys and schoolgirls in bright summer clothes had been brought by their teachers to the railside and stood three and four deep on the platforms. The boys saluted, the girls stood silently gazing.

After the service at Westminster, another train transported Edith's remains to Norwich Thorpe Station. The coffin was put on a gun carriage and escorted to Norwich Cathedral where the Archbishop of Norwich, Dr Bertram Pollock, presided over her burial, interring her remains in a simple grave by the cathedral. Both her memorial dedication and funeral was well attended and additional memorials to her now stand in St Martin's Place in London and in Brussels.

Edith Cavell's memorial in Tombland was unveiled on 12 October 1918. (Norfolk Constabulary Historical Collection)

Edith Cavell's coffin being carried into Norwich Cathedral on 15 May 1919. (Norfolk Constabulary Historical Collection)

Two of Norfolk's sons often come to my mind when I think of the Great War. Both of their stories are very different. The first is Major Lionel John Neville, who died on 17 December 1914 after being grievously wounded near Bailleil on the last day of November. He was cared for at the Casino Hospital in Boulogne and his passing was mentioned in *The Bond of Sacrifice* by L.A. Clutterbuck in 1917:

> In November he was sent to the front to join the 5th Field Company, R.E., and on the last day of the month was transferred to the 50th Company. Within an hour of his arrival on duty in the firing zone at Kemmel he was wounded by a chance bullet, which after passing through his chest lodged in the heart of his brother officer Captain Moores, R.E. He himself chose to be nursed in the Casino Hospital, where he died, that he might himself, as he said, test whether his work there was well done.

Major Neville was buried at Sloley with military honours on 22 December 1914. At this early stage of the war, and due to his standing in life, he numbered amongst the lucky few who were returned to their homes for burial.

Edith Cavell's grave in the grounds of Norwich Cathedral. (Author's collection)

Lionel John Neville's grave in Sloley churchyard. (Author's collection)

One man who did not receive that privilege was Private 26047 Edward Hammond from Shipdham and his is a grave which I have visited on several occasions while conducting battlefield tours. Hammond enlisted in Norwich before initially serving in the Norfolk Yeomanry. However, by April 1918 he was serving on the Western Front with the 8th Battalion East Surrey Regiment. On 4 April 1918, the 18th (Eastern) Division had two brigades – the 53rd and 55th Brigades – in the forward line during the Battle of Villers Bretonneux. The 8/East Surreys were situated to the north of Lance Wood along with the 18th and the 9th Australian Divisions. When three German divisions attacked, they were forced back from their position and it was during this retreat that Edward was posted missing.

The Red Cross investigated the events of that day and a witness was able to report exactly what had happened to Edward. Writing to the Red Cross on 23 September 1918, the witness revealed: 'Early in April at Villers Bretonneux I saw him fall close to me in the open – hit in the back and leg by bullets. We were retiring, and the body was left. I knew him well, he came from Norfolk.'

This information came from Private 5392 Jospeh Cordery, who himself was recovering from wounds in Eastleigh Hospital in Hampshire. By 22 October 1918, the War Office officially accepted that Edward Hammond had been killed in action and buried by Canadian troops. Edward was only 19 years old when he died.

Years later, Tony Hammond saw Edward's death plaque on the mantelpiece above his grandmother's fireplace. Asking her about it, he discovered that she knew very little other than that

The memorial to the fallen of the three Norfolk Field Companies in Norwich Cathedral. (Author's collection)

Edward had been reported missing and it was not known where he was buried. Tony made a promise to his grandmother that he would visit Edward's grave in France, something he managed on 3 November 2008.

Crucifix Corner Cemetery contains 660 Commonwealth, 141 French and two Russian burials and Edward lies within. He is buried close to where he fell and I was able to show Tony the exact spot when he returned once more on 20 May 2012. On both occasions we laid a wreath on Edward's grave, allowing Tony to carry out the promise made to his grandmother. Both days were extremely emotional, even all these years since Edward died.

Edward Hammond's grave at Crucifix Corner Cemetery near Villers-Bretonneux. (Courtesy of Tony Hammond)

This is just one of 2,400 Commonwealth War Graves Commission (CWGC) cemeteries dotted around the world, constructed prior to 1939 as focal points for future generations remembering their fallen relatives. The CWGC believe these cemeteries represent 'churches or cathedrals in which the roof was the sky, the columns the trees and the congregation was both the living and the dead'.

Rudyard Kipling, Sir Edwin Lutyens, Sir Herbert Baker and Sir Reginald Blomfield were all chosen to begin the work of advising, designing and constructing the cemeteries and